A
NEEDLE
in the
RIGHT
HAND
of
GOD

A
NEEDLE
in the
RIGHT
HAND
of
GOD

The Norman Conquest of 1066
and the Making and Meaning
of the Bayeux Tapestry

R. HOWARD BLOCH

RANDOM HOUSE
NEW YORK

Published in the United States by Random House, an imprint of The Random House Publishing Group, a division of Random House, Inc., New York.

RANDOM HOUSE and colophon are registered trademarks of Random House, Inc.

The Bayeux Tapestry is reproduced by special permission of the city of Bayeux.

ISBN-10: 1-4000-6549-6
ISBN-13: 978-1-4000-6549-3

LIBRARY OF CONGRESS CATALOGING-IN-PUBLICATION DATA

Bloch, R. Howard.
A needle in the right hand of God: the Norman conquest of 1066 and the making and meaning of the Bayeux Tapestry/ R. Howard Bloch.
p.   cm.
Includes bibliographical references and index.
ISBN 1-4000-6549-6
1. Bayeux tapestry—History. 2. Hastings, Battle of England, 1066, in art. 3. Great Britain—History—William I, 1066–1087—Historiography. 4. Symbolism in art. I. Title.
NK3049.B3B57 2006
746.44'204338942—DC22
2005057999

Printed in the United States of America on acid-free paper

www.atrandom.com

246897531

FIRST EDITION

Book design by Carole Lowenstein

To
Caroline, Clara,
Louisa, Rebecca,
and Eva

Then William, taking possession of this great victory, was received peacefully by the Londoners, and was crowned at Westminster by Ealdred, archbishop of York. Thus occurred a change in the right hand of God, which a huge comet had presaged at the beginning of the same year. Whence it was said: "In the year one thousand, sixty and six, the English lands saw the flames of the comet."

—HENRY OF HUNTINGTON,
History of the English People, 1133

CONTENTS

PREFACE

I first saw the Bayeux Tapestry when I was twenty. That was before 1983, when it was taken down from its perch around the interior walls of the palace of the bishops of Bayeux, cleaned, photographed (both rear and front), remounted upon a new backing, and placed in a three-sided, angled glass case. Where viewers once stood in the middle of the room, surrounded by the rectangular horseshoe of the Tapestry, they now walk around the outside of the horseshoe as if it were an artifact, albeit a spectacular one, in a museum space. Explanatory panels, projections, audiophones, maps, and dioramas enrich the experience. Light just bright and warm enough to bring out the Tapestry's natural colors more fully than at any time in the past has replaced the old low light associated with the husbanding of electricity in postwar France. All of which means that I caught a glimpse of the last vestige of how the Tapestry might have looked draped around the interior walls of the great hall of a castle or suspended from the piers of the nave of a large church. This was a time when the Tapestry, now considered first and foremost a work of art, may have had a social, political, and even propagandist function as an imposing record of the Norman Conquest of 1066 or, as the first historical mention of the Tapestry in 1476 relates, a liturgical role in the yearly Feast of Relics in Notre-Dame of Bayeux.[1]

The trip to Bayeux was my mother's idea. She grew up in North Carolina, where her formal training as a textile engineer was rounded by the tradition of southern crafts—embroidery, needlework, quilt making—comparable to the arts of the needle of medieval England and Normandy, still known for their embroidery and lace. When we moved north, my mother transformed her native talents into what in the 1950s was called "creative stitchery." Abstract collages assembled from all kinds of materials, from swatches of fabric and thread to ribbon and feathers, laid upon a background of cloth, decorated our walls like the domestic silks, plain tabbies, or embroidered linens found in some homes of the Middle Ages.

My mother and I stayed in Bayeux's Hotel Lion d'Or. I would later learn that this is where, in the summer of 1941, a team of art historians, archaeologists, and artists, sent by Hitler to study the Tapestry, were lodged and fed. After the war, de Gaulle met Churchill at the Lion d'Or, and they shared omelets smothered in legendary Norman butter. So you might say that my first love of the Tapestry came about as a "whirlwind of circumstances"—maternal guidance, the possibility of touching a bit of medieval history along with the living history of World War II into which I was born and which by then was already an intellectual interest, the incredible beauty and power of the Tapestry itself, and eggs. Since then, I have wanted to know more about who designed it, who embroidered it, and where, when, and, in keeping with my mother's preoccupations, how it was actually made.

The story of the sewing of the Tapestry would have delighted my father, who was an expert in the manufacture of finished cloth. Were he still alive, I would have so enjoyed speaking with him about how his eleventh-century equivalent might have gone about finding or commissioning a suitable piece of linen, discussing thread counts and selvage, assessing the dye lots and tex or weight of wool yarn. I can still remember the way he would look closely and rub a piece of worsted between thumb and middle finger, put a match to a fiber or two, hold it to his nostrils, and know the exact composition and weave of the little swatch of cloth whose ragged edges had been cut by pinking shears.

On my last visit to Bayeux, I made an appointment with the Tapestry's current curator, Sylvette Lemagnen, whose official title is "Conservateur de la Médiathèque Municipale et de la Tapisserie de Bayeux." She told me that I would be her first appointment of the morning, and when I arrived at 10:00 A.M., I was shown promptly into the outer office, a high-ceilinged room with long French windows. Five or six women sat at their desks, speaking on the telephone or typing in front of computer screens, while another waited in front of a copier, and still another fed a fax. A printer hummed alongside the bleeps of the answering machine as it delivered the morning's recorded messages. It was a workshop of sorts, what the medievals called a "ladies' chamber," which designated the place where sewing took place. Who knows if these present-day keepers of the Tapestry of Bayeux were not the descendants of the women who had embroidered it over nine centuries ago?

The curator, who was herself completing a doctoral thesis on the Tapestry, informed me right away that there were no unedited documents in the center's archives. I realized that I was probably not the first pesky scholar to enter her office with the hope of uncovering some of its hidden secrets. We chatted amiably about current scholarship and the state of the question of the Tapestry's origins. Was it made right after the Norman Conquest or a little later? Was the idea that of William the Conqueror's wife, Mathilda, or his half-brother Odo? Did it all take place in England or in France? At one point I asked Mme. Lemagnen why the French persisted in calling the Tapestry a tapestry when it was, in fact, an embroidery. A rolling of the eyes and a pouty exhalation were the signs of what I could only imagine to have been something along the lines of "You Americans are sometimes so naïve."

"The mayor of Bayeux would never permit it," she replied.

"The mayor?" I asked.

"Yes," she said. "He is afraid that if you could change the name of the 'Bayeux Tapestry' to the 'Bayeux Embroidery,' the name 'Bayeux' might also someday be changed, and that would mean a loss of tourism for the town." She reminded me that the Tapestry had not always been called thus and that before it was the Bayeux Tapestry, it was Queen Mathilda's Tapestry and, before that, King William's Cloth.

Her response surprised me, since I could not have imagined that a matter as lofty as the name of a famous work of art came down to a question of tourism and money. But, of course. The Tapestry still participates in the medieval tradition by which churches and monasteries guarded the relics of saints and other treasures in order to attract pilgrims along the paths that are the equivalent of today's great tourist routes—Saint Jacques of Compostela in the south and, to the west, Mont-Saint-Michel, which is actually pictured in the Tapestry in its eleventh-century state. From that moment, I began to think of the Tapestry not only as a great work of art, but as a physical object with a long past, including how it disappeared for so many centuries, how it was used to cover a wagon full of munitions during the French Revolution, how it has been pressed into the service of various local interests and national causes since its rediscovery in the 1720s.

As I left the administrative offices of the Centre Guillaume le Conquérant, I was swept along by a sea of English schoolchildren who had crossed the Channel earlier that morning. They were streaming out of several long buses in the parking lot, and as soon as they passed the ticket window, they surrounded the Tapestry so fully that I could hardly see it. Each time I managed to push nearer the glass, which was really too close to see a wide enough swath of the Tapestry to understand the brilliance of its visual flow, I found myself forced again to the rear of a sea of bobbing adolescent heads. One of the things that I have learned about the

Tapestry in the course of study is that it was meant to be looked at in large sweeps that enfold the viewer in what sometimes seems like a three-dimensional space.

I made it around the horseshoe, more or less, and headed from the display room to the bookshop where I had once purchased a long, unfolding reproduction of the Tapestry that has given me much pleasure over the years. This was the best access one could have to it from afar until the appearance in 2003 of the digital edition of the Tapestry on CD, better than the reproduction in books, whose pages, no matter how fast one turns them, never capture the propelling forward movement of the Tapestry's ship launchings, Channel crossings, or cavalry charge. I found one of the books Mme. Lemagnen had recommended. I walked up Bayeux's rue Saint-Jean and stepped into the courtyard of the Lion d'Or. Sitting in front of an omelet that bubbled and bulged as it arrived hot from the kitchen, I remembered that first time and began, there and then, to imagine this little excursion into the medieval past so important in the making of a world that is still recognizably our own.

A
NEEDLE
in the
RIGHT
HAND
of
GOD

CHAPTER I

LANCES, AXES, AND NEEDLES

BAD NEWS REACHED DUKE WILLIAM OF NORMANDY ON THE evening of October 13, 1066. In the two weeks since his spectacular crossing of the Channel in a thousand boats, he had pillaged freely in the English countryside between the old Roman ports of Pevensey and Hastings. Now word came that King Harold had defeated Scandinavian invaders near the town of York and was advancing rapidly from the North. By nightfall, Anglo-Saxons appeared along Senlac ridge, the high ground above the Norman camp. Harold held a strategic advantage over William, who was on unfamiliar terrain. He would be even stronger if reinforcements arrived from London.

William ordered his troops on high alert. Many did not sleep at all that night. Others awoke with the first light, which appeared at 5:20 on the morning of October 14. Sunrise at 6:28 brought an ominous sign. As William dressed for battle surrounded by his most trusted advisers—his half-brothers, Bishop Odo of Bayeux and Count Robert of Mortain, and a company of great Norman and Breton lords—his squires put on his corselet the wrong way around. It was a small thing, but William had confessed his sins the night before and made Communion at the first hour. In a world that believed in dialogue between the human and the divine, it seemed a sign from God. As his attendants struggled to turn the padding beneath his finely woven chain mail and breast armor, William made light of the situation. "We shall turn the strength of my duchy," he joked, "into a kingdom." He lifted the little sack of relics from Odo's extended hand and placed them around his neck, and before Odo had finished praying for victory, William ordered the battle ranks. The duke was steady in the face of unpredictable events. In the crossing of the Channel on the night of September 27, William's ship had arrived before the rest of the fleet. An oarsman reported that "as far as he could see there was nothing but sea and sky." The Norman leader, certain that "all the others would arrive before long," sat down to "an abundant meal, accompanied by spiced wine, as if we were in his hall at home."

The French from France would be on the left, the Bretons on the right, William and the Normans in the center. The archers on foot would open the battle. Set crossbowmen would "pierce the faces of the English with their speeding shafts." The knights on horse would be to the rear of the foot. William pronounced what he knew might be his final words: "Raise your standards, men, and let there be no measure or moderation to your righteous anger. Let the lightning of your glory be seen from the east to the west, let the thunder of your charge be heard, and may you be the avengers of most noble blood."

Great shouting could be heard, the clinking of lifted helmets and mail, the clatter of horses' hooves, and the harsh bray of trumpets on both sides. Dragons could be seen everywhere, on shields and on the banners that caught the wind, as William's army began to array itself as he had ordered. The horsemen and infantry followed the banners to join their battalion; the archers observed them to know by the angle of their flutter how high and in what direction to shoot. The English could not be far off. Through the dust rising from the Norman camp, the forest glittered, full of spears.

Suddenly, one of William's men rode out before the rest. He was not a knight, but a poet by the name of Taillefer, one of the jongleurs the duke had brought with him to entertain the troops. He tossed his sword in the air and began to twirl it in front of the enemy line. Heedless of death, he pricked his horse, which began to charge. He lowered his lance, which pierced an Anglo-Saxon shield, knocking the ax bearer lifeless to the ground. The jongleur severed the head from the prostrate body and, holding it in the air for the Normans to see, began to sing. "The Norman army," in the words of a later chronicler, "struck up the song of Roland to fire them into battle with the example of a heroic warrior." As Taillefer fell, the missiles of war began to fly overhead—arrows, javelins, axes, stones tied to sticks, the square bolts from the crossbows that no shield could resist.

The fighting did not at first go as William planned. The suddenness of the attack left no time for those on foot to place themselves in advance of the mounted knights. Norman archers could not soften Harold's ax-bearing housecarls, the king's personal guard. The knights with lances couched under their arms failed to penetrate the Anglo-Saxon shield wall. In the chaos of the first clash, the rumor circulated that William had been killed. His men broke rank. William quickly decided that he must turn the situation as he had turned his corselet earlier that morning. Drawing upon a tactic that had worked in the past and was well known to the knights who had traveled all the way from southern Italy for the campaign against Harold, the Norman chief joined his fleeing troops until he seemed to be leading the rout. Then, wheeling in his tracks, William raised his visor and showed his face. "Look at me," he cried. "I am alive, and with the aid of God I will conquer. What madness is persuading you to flee? What way is open to escape? The sea lies behind. You will fight to conquer, if you want only to live!" Odo, armed with a club to respect the Christian prohibition against ecclesiastics shedding blood, "rallied the young men."

The Anglo-Saxons rejoiced to see the Normans flee, and, as

William had gambled that he would, Harold charged. The Normans drew the enemy from the high ground. Fanning out and doubling back, they caught the Anglo-Saxon army in a pincer maneuver like that by which Allied forces would trap the German Seventh Army in the Falaise Pocket in August 1944. And the fighting, as in the Battle of Normandy of World War II, was close and fierce. "The dead by falling seemed to move more than the living," recalled one eyewitness. "It was not possible for the lightly wounded to escape, for they were crushed to death by the serried ranks of their companions." William lost three mounts, killed from under him as he fought on horseback and hand-to-hand among his troops. "With his angry blade he tirelessly pierced shields, helmets, and hauberks," writes William's chaplain and biographer, William of Poitiers. "Utterly disdaining fear and dishonor, the Duke charged his enemies and laid them low."

The sun set at 5:04 on October 14, 1066, and at the end of the day, six thousand human corpses, half of those who had ridden, sailed, or walked to Hastings, littered the field alongside six hundred horses. "The mangled bodies that had been the flower of the English nobility and youth covered the ground as far as the eye could see," laments the twelfth-century historian Orderic Vitalis. Harold was dead, so mutilated that his wife was brought to identify his body by "certain marks." Anglo-Saxons who survived their leader made a last stand along a trench known in the eleventh century as the *malfosse,* "bad ditch," into which many Normans, not knowing the terrain, fell and perished without realizing they had won the day. "Many left their corpses in deep woods, many who had collapsed on the routes blocked the way for those who came after. Even the hooves of the horses inflicted punishment on the dead." As the last of Harold's followers vanished into the night, William's army, exhausted, made camp among the fallen of both sides over which he now ruled as king. Having awakened that morning still burdened by the title by which he had always been known, "the Bastard," Duke William went to sleep that night having earned the name history would accord him—"the Conqueror."

The meeting of Normans and Anglo-Saxons at Hastings was the most decisive battle of the Middle Ages and one of the determining days in the making of the West. Hastings changed Britain, which had been dominated since the end of Roman rule by invading tribes from the Continent and the North—Angles, Saxons, and Vikings. This day more than any other turned Britain away from its Scandinavian past and toward Europe. Hastings inaugurated the era of the knight, the social dominance of those who fought with lance on horseback. With the watershed of 1066 came the beginning of the end of the chaos and darkness—the political disintegration and the lack of learning—between the collapse of Charlemagne's empire after his death in the early ninth century and the flowering of state institutions and culture of the Anglo-Norman world. How fitting that the Norman army should enter battle singing of the heroic deeds of Charlemagne's nephew Roland, as if William would begin where the emperor of the Franks had left off. William had himself crowned king of England on Christmas day 1066, just as Charlemagne had been crowned in Rome on Christmas day 800.

If the Battle of Hastings began with poetry, it ended in the realm of the visual arts. The Norman Conquest of England produced the world's most famous textile, the Bayeux Tapestry, a 230-foot-long-by-20-inch-high running embroidered account of the events leading to Hastings and of the battle itself. Made in the decades following the Conquest by those who were party to it, the Tapestry, which contains both images and Latin inscriptions, is a principal source of knowledge about the day that shaped England out of the remains of Anglo-Saxon culture and the Normans, who were themselves relatively recent settlers along the northwest coast of France and the bed of the Seine.

William, only the sixth generation of the Dukes of Normandy, was the descendant of another bold adventurer, the Viking leader Rollo, who in 911 struck a treaty of peace with the French king Charles the Simple by which the old Carolingian territory of Neustria, now weak and ripe for raiding, would be his.

The Tapestry is unique.

Pieces of cloth from the ancient world give some indication of what appealed to the eyes of ancient Persians, Egyptians, and Greeks. Pile carpets from southern Siberia and Turkey, silks from Constantinople, Syria, and China, are dazzling reminders of the riches of the Middle and Far East. Weavings from the bogs of Switzerland, Scandinavia, and East Anglia reveal much about the making of worsteds and tabby beginning with the Celts. Church garments such as the gold- and silk-embroidered handiwork of Saints Herlindis and Relindis, who founded the Abbey of Aldeneik in the eighth century; the stole and girdle that once belonged to the tenth-century saint Cuthbert; and a silk twill coronation robe made for King Roger of Sicily in the 1130s are miraculous survivors of the medieval textile arts. None, however, is on the scale of the Bayeux Tapestry. None possesses its sustained aesthetic quality. None tells a story in images and words. None, in short, captures the essence of an age as vividly as the Bayeux Tapestry, which is for the High Middle Ages what the friezes of Nineveh are for ancient Assyria, the Elgin Marbles are for Greece of the city-state, or the Lady with Unicorn Tapestry is for Renaissance Europe. The only piece of cloth comparable in celebrity to the Bayeux Tapestry is the Shroud of Turin, whose authenticity has been thrown into doubt by radiocarbon dating that suggests it is not the image of a Jewish man crucified in the first century, but a fourteenth-century fabrication.

The Tapestry opens a precious window upon feudalism and knighthood in England and France, political norms and military weaponry and tactics, nautical technique, shipbuilding, and the maritime culture of the North Sea and the English Channel. Its embroidered tableaux reveal much about relations among secular government, ecclesiastical hierarchy, and the papacy; local, baronial, castle, and church architecture; rituals of death, burial, and coronation; hunting and agriculture; customs of eating, cooking, and dress; the material world of sacred and sumptuous objects; and the means of communication and transportation in England, Normandy, and Brittany at the dawn of what Charles Homer Haskins calls the "Renaissance of the Middle Ages."

The story that the Tapestry tells takes place over a period of two years leading up to the Conquest. At its left or beginning edge, we see the ailing king Edward the Confessor (ruled 1042–1066) in counsel with Harold Godwineson, Earl of Wessex and the man who would be king. The interior space may be the royal seat at Winchester, since Westminster Abbey, shown later in the Tapestry, had not yet been consecrated. We know that Edward is frail because of his bodily posture, drooping shoulders, and eyes, and because he has never been well. The Confessor, son of Emma of Normandy and her first husband, King Æthelred II (ruled 978–1016), "the Unready," was a pious man, and things might have gone differently for England if some of the energy he spent praying had been reserved for reproduction. Edward, married to Harold's sister, Edith, was childless, and his bearing at the beginning of the Bayeux Tapestry bespeaks the looming crisis for Anglo-Saxon England. We shall never know the exact nature of Edward's initial exchange with Harold, yet it is hard not to infer that something must have been said about royal succession.

Leaving the audience with Edward, Harold rides to the Godwine ancestral lands in Bosham, where he feasts in the company of retainers. As the feast ends, the Tapestry shows the earl and his men boarding ships for what remains a mysterious trip to the Continent.

Was the purpose of Harold's crossing of the Channel to discuss succession with Duke William of Normandy? A medieval biography of Edward speaks of Harold's traveling abroad "in order to study the French princes." Did Harold visit Normandy to arrange a marriage? His younger brother Tostig had married the sister of Baldwin V of Flanders, father of Duke William's wife, Mathilda, and the twelfth-century historian Orderic Vitalis maintains that Harold, who had married not in church, but only *more danico* ("in the Danish custom"), by cohabitation, sought the hand of one of William and Mathilda's daughters. Orderic's contemporary Eadmer of Canterbury states that Harold sought the release of members of his own family, his brother Wulfnoth and his nephew Hakon, Anglo-Saxon hostages sent to the Norman court at the time of Harold's father's own troubles with King Edward (see p. 16). Still others suggest that Harold did not intend to visit Normandy at all but was en route to Hungary to bring back the most legitimate candidate for kingship, the Æthling Edgar, great-grandson of Æthelred II. The historian William of Malmesbury argues implausibly that Harold was on a fishing expedition when his ship was "blown off-course by a bad wind." Harold was known as a great hunter, and the Tapestry portrays him repeatedly with a falcon on his arm, but fishing was not a noble pursuit in eleventh-century England.

Whatever the reason for Harold's travels, sometime in the fall of 1064 he made landfall near the frontier of upper Normandy. He is shown barefoot and wielding a dagger, indications of shipwreck. The Tapestry thus dramatizes Harold's capture by William's vassal Guy of Ponthieu, who transfers the valuable prisoner to the duke's custody at his court in Rouen.

From Rouen, William and Harold set out on a military expedition to Brittany. While crossing the river Couesnon, Mont-Saint-Michel in the background, Harold is shown bravely rescuing a knight who has slipped into the treacherous mud of the riverbed. William and Harold capture the strongholds of Dol, Rennes, and

Dinan. And as the duke and the earl return to Normandy via Bayeux, William bestows arms on Harold, who swears a sacred oath on relics—not just on relics, but on two reliquaries. The Tapestry captures him, arms outstretched, touching with both hands the jeweled cases that bind him in God's presence to his word. In the epic scenario leading to Hastings, the embroidered image of Harold's swearing is the equivalent of a photograph of what would become his misdeed.

The crux of the Tapestry drama turns around the nature of Harold's oath. Did Harold merely become William's vassal, as the gift of arms and oath of fealty would indicate? Did he make promises regarding the release of hostage family members? Did Harold swear to respect William's rights of succession to the English throne? Was there some kind of understanding involving joint rulership? Was Harold's oath taken willingly or under duress? Was he tricked, as Anglo-Saxon sources suggest? Part of the Tapestry's lasting appeal stems from the fact that alongside the numerous partisan historical accounts by medieval chroniclers on both sides of the Channel, it is not a one-sided version of the events of 1066. In the mold of all enduring works of art, the Tapestry's images, and even its words, make for the richest range of possible meanings.

Having sworn an ill-fated oath, regardless of its actual content, Harold returns to England, where he again meets with King Edward, who looks even more beleaguered than he did at first. As we know from the historical record, Edward died on January 6, 1066, and was buried in Westminster Abbey, England's first Norman Romanesque church, which had been consecrated only two weeks earlier. The Tapestry signals the newness of construction via a figure placing a weathercock on the roof as Edward's bier is carried to its final resting place.

The Tapestry's second act begins with Harold's seizure of the crown the day after Edward's death and the appearance of Halley's comet, which was visible in the skies all over Europe in April 1066, at the Tapestry's upper edge. Harold is depicted with the traditional emblems of imperial power, a scepter and an orb topped with a cross, in the frontal pose of majesty familiar to Roman and Byzantine emperors as well as to Charlemagne and the Ottonians of the tenth century, who saw themselves as the heirs of Rome.

The news of usurpation spreads quickly to Normandy, where William, in council with Odo, orders a fleet to be built in preparation for invasion. The Tapestry discloses in detail the felling of trees for lumber, the shaving and shaping of boats, and the loading of ships with food and wine, arms and armor, and horses prior to William's crossing of the English Channel on the night of September 27. In England, the Normans burn and loot, build earthwork fortifications, scout the countryside. We see them foraging, cooking, and feasting before battle. Both sides reconnoiter and position themselves for the dramatic first clash of battle.

The extraordinary depiction of the chaos and violence of William's engagement with Harold renders the tactical back-and-forth of Norman knights and Anglo-Saxon infantry, of hand-to-hand combat of sword against bearded ax, of lance against shield, of archers and booty seekers, of dead horses and dismembered bodies upon the field of Hastings. The Tapestry ends with a lucky Norman arrow shot through Harold's eye, though we may never know the nature of the final design since the right edge disintegrates in tatters, much like the disarray of the fleeing Anglo-Saxon army after the death of its leader.

Concrete, brutal, vivid—the Tapestry projects a moving image of an important historic event, and every age sees in it its own version of a living, motion-filled past. In our own time, it has been compared to animated comic strips and the moving picture show. For the early nineteenth century, the tapestry was most like the panoramas, precursors to the nickelodeon, that were popular in both England and France. Like the panorama, the cartoon, and the movie, the Tapestry makes history come alive. The story it tells revolves around two of the most powerful of medieval men, whose ambitions and capacities make their meeting at Hastings seem inevitable.

Born in the town of Falaise in 1027 or 1028, William was the illegitimate child of Duke Robert I and a "girl of that town." Robert, according to medieval sources, saw Herlève washing clothes in a stream near the castle and immediately fell in love with the tanner's daughter, with whom he conceived a child when he was no older than seventeen. William's parents never married, though Robert later arranged a union between Herlève and the Viscount of Conteville. Their two sons, Odo of Bayeux and Robert of Mortain, accompanied William on the Conquest and figure prominently among the Tapestry's principal actors. In 1035, Duke Robert left Normandy for the Holy Land, a pilgrimage from which he never returned.

Before his departure for the Middle East, Robert elicited from his vassals a promise to protect and support his son William, then only seven. Some kept their word, while others profited from William's minority to seize what they could while the duchy remained leaderless. It may, in fact, have been William's humble origins that account for his survival. Appealing to the members of Robert's former household, moving constantly throughout Normandy, hiding her son in peasant cottages, Herlève used her wiles, wiles associated to this day with the French peasantry, and her knowledge of the reaches of the countryside to protect William from attack by Norman nobles and even by the king of France.

Before long, William began to protect himself. At the age of nineteen, he defeated rebellious barons outside of Caen and forced them to swear in the presence of clerics and on holy relics a Truce of God, prohibiting private war from Wednesday evening until Monday morning and during the seasons of Advent, Lent, Easter, and Pentecost. It was the beginning of the medieval peace movement and the beginning of William's pacification of the duchy over which he would in the following decade gradually gain control.

"A warrior age salutes a warrior, and in the young William it found a warrior to salute," writes William's biographer David Douglas. William was a brilliant military leader, defeating even the French king Henry I at the Battle of Mortemer in 1054. It was after Mortemer that Guy of Ponthieu, who captured Harold, became William's vassal. Yet the duke was also a savvy political strategist who understood the importance of an alliance with the church. An anonymous monk of Caen, who may actually have seen William, describes him as a balance between the medieval ideals of strength and wisdom: "a burly warrior with a harsh guttural voice, great in stature but not ungainly. He was temperate in eating and drinking. . . . After his meal he rarely drank more than thrice. In speech he was fluent and persuasive, being skilled at all times in making clear his will." William reversed the Viking practice of sacking religious institutions, and alongside the castle building and fortification of the type depicted in the Bayeux Tapestry, he built monasteries, abbeys, churches, and cathedrals and supported ecclesiastical reform. A hundred years before the accession of William, probably not a monastery survived in the region of Rouen. At the time of the Conquest, Normandy was renowned for its abundance of religious houses that benefited directly from ducal patronage. So, too, the duke profited from the knowledge of accounting put to use in the administration of his expanding duchy by clerics who knew how to read and write.

The Norman church was reorganized under a strong set of bishops who cooperated with the duke. The duke, in turn, cooperated with the pope. In preparation for the invasion of England,

William summoned his vassals to swear loyalty in his absence. He met with the young Philip I, king of France, who was at the time under the tutelage of William's father-in-law, Count Baldwin V of Flanders. He dispatched envoys to the court of the king of Germany and future emperor of Rome, Henry IV (ruled 1056–1106). But, most important, William sent a mission to Pope Alexander II, who bestowed his blessing upon a Norman crossing of the Channel. William went into battle on the morning of October 14, 1066, with the papal banner and, around his neck, the consecrated relics on which Harold had sworn. If Hastings was a brilliant and brave military triumph that seemed at times to hang by a thread, even that thread would have snapped were it not for the months of local and pan-European preparation, much of which is visible in the Tapestry, prior to the event.

As precarious as William's minority and accession to power had been, the route by which Harold Godwineson came to power in England was just as perilous, though he might at the outset have appeared predestined to rule. The Godwine family came to prominence during the final years of the reign of Æthelred II as the kingdom faced the threat of Viking raids. Harold's father, Godwine, survived the death of Æthelred in 1016 and was appointed to high office by his successor, King Cnut (ruled 1016–1035), to whom he was also related by marriage. In the crisis of succession after Cnut's death, Godwine is suspected of having had the future king Edward's older brother Alfred blinded and murdered in the first attempt of Æthelred's sons by Emma to return from Normandy, where they had been in exile during the rule of Cnut. When Cnut's son King Hardecnut died in 1042, Edward came home to England and initially relied upon Godwine to secure and preserve his throne. Relations between Edward and Godwine were never easy, however, and in 1051 the king declared Godwine an outlaw, repudiated his daughter, Edith, and gave him just five days safe conduct to leave England. The king confiscated Wessex, which at the time consisted of almost all the territory south of the Thames. It is possible, too, that at this time Edward promised his succession to William, who, according to *The Anglo-Saxon Chronicle,* visited King Edward while the Godwines were away. William's chaplain and biographer, William of Poitiers, states that the offer was made in gratitude for the refuge afforded Edward in his early years and came with the assent of English nobility.

Godwine, his wife, Gytha, and their sons Sweyn, Tostig, and Gyrth crossed to Flanders, while his other sons, Harold and Leofwine, went to Bristol to recruit mercenaries. There they were received by Diarmait Mac Mael-Na-Mbo, king of Leinster, who held the Viking city of Dublin, to which Harold's sons would flee after Hastings. Nobles turned outlaws, Harold and Leofwine raided along the south coast of England. By 1052, they sailed up the Thames, forcing Edward to restore the Godwine lands in Wessex, to take back Edith, and to replace the Norman Robert of Jumièges, whom Edward had installed as archbishop of Canterbury, with Stigand, who is pictured in the Bayeux Tapestry alongside Harold in the scene of his coronation. Godwine's son and grandson Wulfnoth and Hakon were sent as hostages to Normandy to guarantee the agreement, since Edward, who had grown up there, trusted Norman nobles more than many of his own countrymen.

When Harold Godwineson succeeded his father as Earl of Wessex in 1053, he was the wealthiest man in the kingdom. According to the Domesday Book, which William ordered compiled in 1086 based on the living memory of landholdings in 1066, the Godwine family held estates valued for tax at 5,187 pounds, while King Edward personally held only 3,840 pounds. For the nine months and nine days he was king of England, Harold combined the ancestral Godwine lands with royal possessions.

Adventurous, resolute, aggressive, brutal, and brilliant tacticians, willing to risk all for the sake of a kingdom, William and Harold lived by the law of the strongest in a world in which the death of a ruler more often than not brought a bitter struggle for succession. How is it, then, that their story was captured not in the marble or bronze of ancient heroic monuments, but in the simple medium of embroidered wool on linen, the work most likely of women? The question goes right to the heart of the drama depicted in the Bayeux Tapestry and underscores the role of art in the conversion of a factional and tribal society founded in violence into a society governed by something like the rule of law.

Great works of art are often the repository of dreams. As a visual record of the Conquest, the Tapestry was a powerful vehicle of cultural memory at a time when even the most powerful lords were illiterate. Not only a means by which future generations might learn of the event, the world's most famous textile worked to forge a community in which conquerors and conquered might someday fuse into a single people with shared interests and values. Warring factions continued to contest the rulership of England long after the Conquest. Yet, as we shall see in the pages that follow, the Tapestry is a voracious cultural artifact, absorbing and weaving together all who were party to the historical trauma of 1066.

There may be something physiological in the workings of the eye and the neurological space behind the eye in our perception of a work of art whose appeal has lasted as long as that of the Tapestry. And even if the appeal is not physiological, something so profound and shaping happened in the decades following 1066 that we are no longer able to see it clearly: It is simply part of our perceptual universe.

The Bayeux Tapestry is a means of understanding the High Middle Ages. It reflects and unlocks the world around it, captures a cultural moment and anticipates historical change, embodies and models understandings and institutions at a critical time in the formation of English culture out of the disparate threads of the Anglo-Saxon, Scandinavian and Viking, Norman, and Continental cultures and even vestiges of the late Roman and Mediterranean worlds. Part of the enduring effect of the Tapestry, which is monumental in its own right, has to do with the power to integrate so much and so fully the various strands of imagery and meaning available at the time of its creation. In this, the Tapestry is the artistic birth certificate of what is sometimes referred to as the "Norman miracle" and of our own sense of the shape of the past.

The Tapestry is an icon of the Middle Ages. Alongside the great cathedrals like Notre Dame, Canterbury, and Chartres; famed castles like the Tower of London or Chinon; legendary lovers like Abelard and Heloise or Tristan and Iseult; heroes and heroines like Richard "the Lionheart" or Joan of Arc; poets and intellectuals like Dante or Thomas Aquinas; saints like Bernard or Francis; mythical figures like Robin Hood, Arthur, Lancelot, and Guinevere; fabulous objects like Excalibur, the Round Table, and the Holy Grail; and the musical rhythms of Gregorian chants or the *Carmina Burana,* the Tapestry is deeply entwined in the popular imagination with what "medieval" means. It has appeared on the cover of books, in comics, in video games, and in movies, beginning with the 1958 Richard Fleischer film *The Vikings.* The heroine Jimena is featured embroidering the Bayeux Tapestry in Anthony Mann's 1961 *El Cid,* as are Ophelia in Franco Zeffirelli's 1990 *Hamlet* and Lady Marion in Kevin Reynolds's 1991 *Robin Hood: Prince of Thieves.* The Tapestry appears on the wall of De Bracy's castle in the Classic Comics Illustrated version of *Ivanhoe* and in the background of the child's animated version of Brian

Jacques's *Redwall*. It is featured on countless trinkets, household knickknacks, and clothes—on mugs, dish towels, sampler-size embroideries, decorative banners, pillows, scarves, T-shirts, and ties. Put to parodic or comic use, the Tapestry returns as travesty. To commemorate the new millennium, Bayer AG produced a running history of the Bayer Corporation—"the Bayer Tapestry"—from the founding of the chemical company in 1860 to the acquisition of Monsanto in 1995 and Chiron Diagnostics in 1999. A *New Yorker* cartoon of 1991 shows a man wearing what appears to be a 230-foot-long tie with a reproduction of the Tapestry trailing behind him and around the corner. Underneath, the caption reads, "Bayeux Tie."

The "Bayeux Tie" was not the first notice in *The New Yorker*. The cover of the July 15, 1944, issue acknowledged D-Day, just five weeks earlier, with a brilliant rendering of the crossing and landing of Allied troops on the beaches of Normandy in the format, style, and colors of the Bayeux Tapestry (see insert, figure 1). In the place of King Edward and Harold, we see King George, Roosevelt, and Churchill; in the place of Duke William and Odo, we see General Eisenhower and Field Marshal Montgomery (whose ancestors came to England with the Conquest); in the place of the Tapestry's Viking boats, Allied ships and planes cross the English Channel; and in the bottom panels, Allied soldiers and tanks chase surrendering Germans across Norman fields as Hitler, hands in the air, emerges from a bunker whose architecture reproduces, as if a tracing, the building in which the treacherous Harold sits after his coronation. Even the Tapestry's decorative borders, filled, as we shall see, with exotic animals, floral designs, and scenes from everyday life, translate into the American eagle, a face and microphone of the Free French, a handshake across the sea, fish, submarines, and land mines, and, under the scene of Hitler's surrender, fleeing rats. The inscriptions, in the block capitals of the Tapestry's epigraphic Latin, read

GEORGE REX: ABSIT INVIDIA: MONTY ET IKE: MARE NAVI-
GAVIT: D-DAY·JVNE VI A·D·M·C·M·X·L·IV: BAYEUX JVNE VII:
SIC SEMPER TYRANNIS—KING GEORGE: PUT QUARRELS ASIDE:
MONTY AND IKE: CROSSES THE SEA: D-DAY·JUNE 6 AD 1944:
BAYEUX JUNE 7: THIS IS HOW IT GOES WITH TYRANTS.

Rea Irvin, the cartoonist and the first art director of *The New
Yorker,* shows considerable knowledge of the situation of the Allied forces in the spring of 1944. The enigmatic PUT QUARRELS
ASIDE: MONTY AND IKE refers no doubt to the tension between
Generals Montgomery and Eisenhower. But he had no way of
knowing that the leaders of the Third Reich were fascinated by
the Bayeux Tapestry. It is to that story and to the history of the
Tapestry since its discovery in the early eighteenth century that
we now turn.

CHAPTER 2

PERILS
AND
SURVIVAL

EARLY IN THE MORNING OF JUNE 4, 1941, JUST OVER A YEAR after the invasion and occupation of France, four men entered a car in Berlin and were driven west. They were followed by a truck bearing not the matériel of war, but seven cases, almost a ton, of photographic and artistic equipment and supplies. Though none was by training a member of the SS, each bore a title and wore the gray uniform of Hitler's elite troops in order that they might cross the border more easily—SS Sturmbannführer Herbert Jankuhn, professor of history and curator of prehistoric antiquities at the museum of Kiel; SS Unterscharführer Schlabow, director of the museum of the history of traditional Germanic costume at Neumünster; and SS Sturmbannführer Alber and SS Mann Herbert Jeschke, a photographer and a painter, both from Berlin. They reached Paris in a little over twenty-four hours. There they conferred with military authorities for almost two days before leaving for Normandy, where they were expected at Bayeux's Hotel Lion d'Or.

The next morning there were negotiations, first with Maître Dodeman. The mayor had not been informed of the plan to move the little group's activities from Bayeux to the château of Monceaux. He mumbled something about a "fire hazard" and insisted on consulting the ministère des beaux-arts. M. Le Prunier, a local professional photographer, was called to provide supplementary photographic material. But Professor Jankuhn, head of the mission, was disappointed with what he saw in M. Le Prunier and exasperated that the Agfa plates they had brought with them did not seem to fit the camera at hand. He made a quick trip to Paris to ask for the services of a specialist in color photography and a close-up lens.

On June 13, Jankuhn could wait no longer. He ordered the heavy sealed canister to be brought from its concrete bunker in the cellar of the Bishop's Palace. The canister was opened, and a long piece of cloth, smelling noticeably of insecticide, was removed and rolled between two wooden bobbins. This was the procedure that M. Falue, steward of the Bishop's Palace, used whenever German officers (and there had been many lately) pulled up to Bayeux's Town Hall in a black Mercedes or Citroën or even on motorcycle and demanded to see *der Teppich.*

Vault in which the Bayeux Tapestry was stored during World War II
PHOTO COURTESY OF EMMANUEL BRÉARD, CAMARA BAYEUX

Jankuhn's visit was different from those of the others. He came with orders directly from Germany's minister of the interior, Heinrich Himmler, and perhaps even from Reichsführer Hitler himself. Himmler established a research group, Das

Ahnenerbe, for the purpose of preserving useful cultural heritage, and he was directly responsible for the Jankuhn mission, which was to photograph it, paint it, and study its meaning for the Third Reich. As an account of a great battle won by a great Scandinavian, William the Conqueror, whose ancestors were relatively recent settlers from the North, the Tapestry was an example of original Germanic art, not the "degenerate art" that Hitler had assembled, exposed, and sold off in Switzerland several years earlier. And like his plans for the new Teutonic empire, it had endured for almost a thousand years.

Jankuhn, a specialist in Viking culture, must have shivered at that first glimpse. It was like a photograph from the eleventh century, of the horses and men, the costumes and arms, the ships and buildings, of the Viking world. How could he have failed to imagine the Führer as the last in the line of conquerors whose legacy was still alive in that very room? From all that he had read to prepare for this day, Jankuhn knew that the bishop of Bayeux at the time of the Conquest, William's half-brother Odo, was most likely the one who had ordered the Tapestry in the first place. That was before Odo's ambition got him into trouble and William had him imprisoned, some say, because Odo wanted to be pope.

On June 17, Jankuhn, Dr. Hörmann, a representative of the Kunstschutz beim OKM, the military service charged with the mission of protecting works of art, M. Dupont, a French government inspector of historical monuments, M. Falue, and an interpreter drove to the château of Monceaux. They concluded it was, just as the mayor had said, "not immune from the threat of fire." Monceaux was not a suitable place for serious study. The group set out for the monastery at Juaye-Mondaye, ten kilometers from Bayeux, where it was agreed they would work—every day from 9:00 A.M. until 9:00 P.M.—beginning on June 23 until August 1. Three customs agents would be lodged in the monastery under the supervision of M. Falue to guard the Tapestry day and night. On the night of June 19, Professor Jankuhn, unable to wait, ordered a few pictures to be taken in the bishop's palace under a photographic lamp that had also traveled all the way from Berlin. The Tapestry, accompanied by a German motorcycle guard "armed from head to foot," was transported from Bayeux to Mondaye on the morning of June 22. On June 26, two military policemen posted signs on the monastery door prohibiting entrance by occupation troops.

German art historians examining the Bayeux Tapestry
PHOTO COURTESY OF EMMANUEL BRÉARD, CAMARA BAYEUX

For some time before the Jankuhn mission to Bayeux, the leaders of the Third Reich had been interested in original artifacts to substantiate claims to racial purity. As early as 1936, Hitler and Himmler tried to bring back to Berlin a fifteenth-century manuscript of Tacitus's *Germania*. Written in the first century, Tacitus's account of the meeting of Roman and northern civilizations was considered "the birth certificate of the German race." At first, the Reich's efforts to remove the *Germania* from its home in the Balleani family library in Fontedamo, Italy, to its "natural homeland" in Berlin were thwarted by Mussolini, who sought to keep it as a monument to Roman imperial claims. But after the downfall of Mussolini, and as late as the fall of 1943, Hitler sent a convoy of SS officers to search for Tacitus's text, which they failed to discover in its hiding place in the kitchen cellar of the nearby Balleani castle of Iesi.[1]

In the spirit of Tacitus's *Germania,* the leaders of the Reich saw the Bayeux Tapestry as a visual record of Teutonic ingenuity and daring. And so, standing before the unfurled embroidery, the professor and the artist focused their attention upon the most dramatic scenes, such as the launching of a fleet of ships to conquer England from a spot on the Norman coast not too far from where they presently stood. That was just two weeks before the Battle of Hastings, which changed the history of England and brought a new order to Europe—and could not have failed to resonate with the new order so much on the minds of everyone in the room.

Himmler's goal was twofold. He was responding to complaints from both the French and Germans that so many officers of the occupation force had demanded to see the Tapestry that the object itself was being harmed by all the unrolling and rerolling. The authorities decided that it would be studied for some reasonable amount of time, photographed, and described, then removed to one of the safe depositories for national artworks, the château of Sourches, in the department of Sarthe in the Loire Valley near Le Mans. Himmler was interested in finding in the Tapestry the origins of the German state in the Norman state of Sicily and in Normandy itself. Reich leaders had read the biography of Kaiser Frederick II (1194–1250) published in 1931 by a young historian, Ernst Kantorowicz. They admired in the medieval German king and Roman emperor, whose mother, Constance of Sicily, was a Norman, the dream of uniting Germany with the South. A document entitled "The Dossier on Research of the Society of Das Ahnenerbe Concerning the Bayeux Tapestry" makes the claim as early as July 8, 1939, that "this masterpiece has especially for us considerable value. The Tapestry shows that the heritage and the customs of Vikings from Scandinavian countries continued to live in Normandy in a relatively pure form. We must study in depth certain details, particularly the arms, the equipment, and the costumes, in order to date and to prove its Norman origin." Further, "Scientific study and interpretation of events will," it was hoped in the early days of the occupation, when Hitler was thinking of crossing the English Channel, "give supplementary information about the invasion of England by the Normans."[2]

Jankuhn, who had worked previously on the Celtic dig at Haithabu, Schleswig, had been selected as the man most qualified to lead the team that would study the Tapestry. And study they did. Alber, the photographer, made three trips to Paris to develop his color negatives and to buy more plates. When he left Mondaye on June 30, 1941, he had photographed the Tapestry in its entirety. Nonetheless, Jankuhn engaged another photographer, Frau Uhland of the Kunstwissenschaftlichen Institut (Art Institute) of Marburg, to replace Alber. The arrival of a woman in the monastery so shocked the monks of Mondaye that they insisted the table, specially constructed for the little group's work, be moved along with all the photographic and artistic equipment and the Tapestry itself from the upper floors to the ground floor, which was more suitable for guests.

In her pains to be thorough, Frau Uhland carefully removed the thread basting that attached the original Tapestry to its backing, which had been placed there sometime between the sixteenth and the eighteenth centuries, and photographed portions of the embroidered stitching from the rear. Meanwhile, SS Loeb, a military reporter, made two documentary films to be shown as newsreels, and Jeschke, the painter, produced watercolor drawings of many of the details and the scenes of the Tapestry—the figure-heads of the boats, dress, shields, dragons in the margins, the so-called portal of Ælfgyva, banners, and helmets—which, as we shall see, are most illustrative of the Viking world. On July 15, 1941, Count Metternich, German officer, curator of historic monu-ments in the Rhenish region, and chief of the Scientific Mission for the Preservation of Historic Monuments of France, arrived on a tour of inspection. Professor Jankuhn assured him that the study team would wrap up its work by the end of the month.

When Jankuhn left Bayeux on August 5, 1941, he took with him some twelve cases of research material, 426 black-and-white and color photographs (plus 351 doubles), precise measurements and a description of the Tapestry in its most minute detail, enough samples of the thread to conduct "controlled experi-ments," and a journal filled with the pleasures and frustrations of everyday life in occupied Bayeux—the difficulty of finding a car to take him to Mondaye, the goodwill of the monks, electricity outages that hindered the photographic work, and the excellent dinners prepared by the owner of the Lion d'Or, after which he listened to the news reports broadcast from the general head-quarters of the Führer.[3] Jankuhn was surprised to learn on June 22, 1941, that Hitler had invaded Russia, for he must have real-ized that the opening of an eastern front would defer, if not can-cel, any thought of invading Great Britain.

By August 8, Jankuhn was back in Kiel making arrangements for Loeb's documentary film to be the centerpiece of an arts fes-tival inaugurated by the Reichsführer and for the edition of a four-volume collective work by historians, ethnologists, literary specialists, and architects on all aspects of the Tapestry to be pub-lished in a series entitled the History of Art in Western Europe. Though the book never appeared, the members of Jankuhn's scholarly team conducted extensive discussions about the political versus the religious nature of the Tapestry in an orchestrated attempt to establish its Germanic origins. Professor Jankuhn read a paper entitled "The Conquest of England by the Normans, According to the Bayeux Tapestry" to Himmler's circle of friends in Berlin in April 1943 and another at the academy in Stettin in August of that same year.[4]

The Bayeux Tapestry was again sprayed with naphthalene to prevent damage by moths, replaced in its waterproof lead cylinder, and transported on August 19 from Bayeux to the château of Sourches. There had been negotiations about where to find the twenty-five gallons of gas necessary for the 350-kilometer round trip, and Maître Dodeman's appeal directly to Count Metternich had met with a negative response. A local merchant volunteered his ancient gas-generator delivery truck, which, early in the morning of August 18, 1941, was loaded with a dozen sacks of coal to be converted to combustible fuel. The three men who accompanied the Tapestry had to get out and push their valuable load up steep hills, the truck would not restart after lunch, and it broke down several times en route. The drivers, with permission from the authorities for only a one-day trip, would not make it back that night. They found lodging thanks to the caretaker of the City Hall of Alençon, where all the hotels were full with refugees evacuated by the Germans for "mysterious reasons" from the Norman coast. When the drivers returned to Bayeux at 11:30 the next morning, they were, according to one eyewitness, "fatigued and all covered with soot." Mayor Dodeman of Bayeux wrote a letter of gratitude to the mayor of Alençon.[5]

The Tapestry did not remain undisturbed for very long. At the end of 1943, Jeschke, the painter, was granted permission to visit Sourches for the purpose of making more drawings. And as late as July 6, 1944, fully a month after Allied troops had landed on the beaches of Normandy, SS Sievers of Himmler's Ahnenerbe Heritage Bureau ordered in the name of the Reichsführer that "this important Germanic monument" be moved from France to an SS bunker in Berlin.

Why didn't Hitler simply seize the Bayeux Tapestry in 1941 when he had the chance? Perhaps he didn't because he wished to leave this early artifact of Nordic culture upon French soil as a marker, a claim of the Teutonic presence dating back to a time even before the creation of nation-states. In any event, by the time he got around to it, it was too late. As Allied troops pressed toward Paris in August 1944, German press and radio reported the false news that the Bayeux Tapestry had fallen into the hands of an American antiques dealer. And only in February 1945 did German authorities discover that on June 27, just after the Allied landing in Normandy, the Tapestry was transferred under the auspices of the German Commission for the Protection of French Artworks to the basement of the Louvre.

On August 21, 1944, in the middle of the street fighting between French partisans and the German occupiers of Paris, two men in SS uniforms and a truck "stuffed with containers of gas when fuel was in short supply everywhere" presented themselves to General Von Choltitz, commander in chief of the German army of the capital, who in a later account reports that they delivered a command:[6]

> —Orders from the *Reichsführer SS,* Herr General, we have come to remove the Bayeux Tapestry to Berlin.
>
> —What good luck, replied Von Choltitz, you want to place it out of harm's way?
>
> —Ja, Herr General.
>
> —I'm very glad. Would you please follow me out on the balcony.
>
> The three of us looked at the Louvre directly across the way. Projectiles were falling thick and fast. From the rooftop an enemy machine gun began to fire in the direction of the Seine.

—You see, I said, the tapestry is there, in the basement of the Louvre.

—But, Herr General, the Louvre is occupied by the enemy! replied one of the SS.

—Of course it is occupied, and heavily too. . . .

—But, under these conditions, Herr General, how can we take possession of the tapestry?

—Messieurs, I said, you are the leaders of the best soldiers in the world. I will put five or six of my best men at your disposal and will cover you as you cross the rue de Rivoli. You need only capture one door and, fighting your way in, carry it off.

The two SS hesitated, then one found a way out.

—Herr General, the French government has no doubt already removed the tapestry?

—Not at all, the tapestry is there, but you will have to seize it by force. . . .

"I had evaluated the two men correctly," Von Choltitz notes. "When one has served long in the army one learns to distinguish a soldier from a mere wearer of a uniform. I got rid of the two messengers of the *Reichsführer* and never saw them again."

The Tapestry was exhibited in Paris in the fall of 1944 before returning to the Bishop's Palace of Bayeux. From there it was transferred to the former Grand Seminary, remodeled to house the Municipal Library and Centre Guillaume le Conquérant after a cleaning and restoration in 1982–1983. One observer of this final reinstallation claimed in an article entitled "The Bayeux Tapestry Still Smells" that the Tapestry retained the odor of insecticide, the last vestige of its time in hiding during World War II.[7]

Part of the aura surrounding the Tapestry has to do with its longevity. In the middle of the nineteenth century, the French poet Théophile Gautier exclaimed: "How remarkable that this fragile strip of linen should have come down to us undamaged through the centuries when so many strong buildings have fallen into ruins!"

The Tapestry is a survivor.

Hitler was not the first to be fascinated by the Bayeux Tapestry and to want to use the images of war to make war. The Tapestry was born in armed conflict, and it has elicited strong militaristic and patriotic feelings in times of great national and international upheaval. Like any major work of art from the ancient or medieval world, it has a tale to tell.

The Tapestry has known periods of shining in the spotlight and of obscurity. From the time of its creation in the years following the Conquest of 1066, it left no trace whatsoever until an inventory of goods of the Bayeux Cathedral compiled in 1476 mentions "a very long and narrow curtain embroidered with images and writing which show the Norman conquest of England." This is all there is before the Tapestry emerged from the mists of time and entered the historical record with the publication in 1729 of a presentation that the French historian Antoine Lancelot made to the Académie Royale des Inscriptions et Belles-Lettres in 1724 in which he spoke of a drawing made by a friend of a "monument of William the Conqueror." The drawing had left him baffled: "In spite of all my endeavors, I have, up to the present, been unable to discover whether this sketch represents a bas-relief or a sculpture round the choir of a church or a tomb; whether it is a fresco, a painting on the glass of several windows, or, possibly, a tapestry."[8]

Lancelot's article provoked the interest of a monk of the Congregation of Saint-Maur, Paris, the classical scholar Dom Bernard de Montfaucon, who wrote to a fellow Benedictine,

Dom Romain de La Londe, prior of Saint Stephen's in Caen, Normandy. From de La Londe, Montfaucon learned that the sketch was indeed the first part of a tapestry. The drawing was made by Anne Foucault, daughter of Nicolas-Joseph Foucault, governor of Normandy from 1689 to 1704 and a collector of antiquities. It was found among his papers after his death in 1721. Thus, when the first volume of an inventory of royal monuments appeared in 1729, plates XXXV–XLIX contained images engraved from Anne Foucault's original drawings.[9] Montfaucon, meanwhile, dispatched a draftsman to copy the rest, which appeared in volume II of the *Monumens de la Monarchie Française* along with what may be considered the first essay on the Tapestry, attributing it to William's wife, Mathilda, who, Lancelot maintained, commissioned it shortly after 1066.[10]

For most of its existence, the Tapestry lay quietly rolled upon the winchlike device on which it was apparently stored from time beyond memory until the middle of the nineteenth century, either in Notre-Dame of Bayeux, the bishop's palace, or the Municipal Library. It was visited at first by what were known before the birth of the discipline of archaeology as "antiquarians," amateurs, connoisseurs, and collectors interested for the most part in local history or in family genealogies. Antiquarian curiosity led, in fact, to discovery of many of the manuscripts of the Middle Ages, neglected by the Renaissance and by the neoclassicism of the seventeenth century, which turned to ancient Greece and Rome and averted its eyes from the medieval past, from "the time of the Goths," in the phrase of Renaissance writer François Rabelais. In prerevolutionary France, as in England to this day, medieval manuscripts were often still housed in the castles of their ancestral owners.

Once a year, during the Feast of Relics and the Octave of Saint John, a liturgical period of eight days in July, the Tapestry was unrolled and hung around the nave of the cathedral, as we

Engraving from 1824 of the winch on which the Bayeux Tapestry was wound

FROM THOMAS FROGNALL DIBDIN, *A BIBLIOGRAPHICAL ANTIQUARIAN AND PICTURESQUE TOUR IN FRANCE AND GERMANY* (LONDON: ROBERT JENNINGS AND JOHN MAJOR, 1829)

know from a series of letters published between 1730 and 1732 by the antiquarian Jean de la Roque, who visited Bayeux some fifteen years earlier. So, too, we know that the Tapestry was seen in 1746 by an English antiquarian, William Stukeley, and in 1752 by Andrew Ducarel, who confirms the report of an annual exhibition in July. But for the most part, the Tapestry lay dormant upon its roller until it was put on permanent display and began to attract the tourists who in the middle of the nineteenth century replaced the antiquarians and connoisseurs of an earlier era.

On several occasions before Hitler's attempt to seize it, the Tapestry was the focal point of national and international drama and fell into considerable risk. In the aftermath of the French Revolution, which relegated the possessions in libraries and cathedrals to "communal destruction," it narrowly escaped catastrophe when a local military contingent from Bayeux wrapped one of its equipment wagons in an "old piece of cloth resting in the Cathedral." Only at the last minute did a lawyer by the name of Lambert Léonard Leforestier obtain a legal injunction that he waved before the unruly crowd, which backed off. Léonard Leforestier removed the Tapestry to his own office in the Commissary of Police in return for his promise to furnish a canvas substitute.

In 1794, under a movement to preserve national treasures menaced by the Terror of 1793, the Tapestry was "nationalized" and became public property as an antiquity in the care of the National Commission for the Arts. On 10 Ventôse, year II, (February 23, 1794), the local commissioners saved it once again from being cut into pieces to decorate a revolutionary float. This time, however, they tried to make its protection permanent with a letter to the mayor:

> Our task, Citizen, embracing, as it does, the investigation of everything of interest to Public Education, we cannot neglect an object, the possession of which was considered an honor for our community under the Ancien Régime. The conquest of England by the Normans has long been a matter of personal pride to us. Today, when all parts of the Republic are united where national wealth and glory are concerned, the record of the Conquest has become public property...we must therefore request you to inform us of the place at which the Tapestry is stored so that we may effect its removal to one of the depots in this district.[11]

In August of that year, the Tapestry was removed from the sacristy of the cathedral and unrolled in the "Temple of the Supreme Being," a government depot. At that time, too, its condition was assessed by a comparison with the original drawings published by Montfaucon.

Napoleon, contemplating an invasion of England, had the Tapestry put on display in the Musée Napoléon in Paris between

November 1803 and February 1804. It is from this exhibition that the Bayeux Tapestry, known until then as the Tapestry of Duke William, received its second name, imposed by the director-general of French museums: *la tapisserie brodée de la reine Mathilde*—Queen Mathilda's Tapestry. The emperor, then only first consul, was reported to have studied it and been so impressed by the parallel between a comet observed in France and southern England shortly after the installation and the "hairy star" depicted in the Tapestry to signal the relation between Harold's coronation and William's crossing of the Channel that a description was printed in the guide to the exhibition: "Dover, December 6, 1803. Last night about five o'clock we observed a superb comet which rose in the south-west and moved towards the north: it had a tail about thirty yards long. The whole countryside was lighted for many miles around, and after it disappeared, one smelled a strong odour of sulphur."[12]

The Tapestry, for the first time a national rather than a local object, captured the imagination of the French public. The exhibition in the capital inspired a play at the Théâtre du Vaudeville, *La Tapisserie de la Reine Mathilde,* which, in contrast with the drama of invasion, featured women alternately embroidering and praying onstage for the success of their warrior husbands.[13]

Upon its return from Paris to Bayeux, the Tapestry, still preserved on an enormous pulleylike roller from which it was unwound and rewound for viewing, received a number of visitors. The most diligent was Charles Stothard, a British artist dispatched in 1818 by the Society of Antiquaries of London for the purpose of making a detailed full-size color reproduction. Stothard spent two years sketching the Tapestry, at the end of which, comparing his drawing with that of Montfaucon, he concluded that the crude method of storing it would mean that "in the course of a few years, the means of accomplishing" what he had done "would no longer exist."[14] Stothard apparently knew of what he spoke, since during the period he was sketching, a piece of the Tapestry was removed, later turning up in the Victoria and Albert Museum, London, where it was exhibited until its return in 1871. Mrs. Stothard had been suspected of the theft, a suspicion countered by one of Mrs. Stothard's nephews, who claimed that Mr. Stothard already possessed two pieces of the Tapestry at the time of their marriage.[15] Stothard's and others' warnings about deterioration were taken seriously, however, and the Tapestry was removed in 1842 to a room in the Bibliothèque Publique, where it was unwound and exhibited behind glass. Since that time, the Tapestry has been absent only three times from public view: once during the Franco-Prussian War of 1870 under fear of a German invasion of Normandy; again at the outbreak of World War II; and, finally, for the examination and restoration of 1982–1983.

Was the Bayeux Tapestry intended originally for a religious or a secular purpose? Was it meant to hang in a great cathedral or a princely hall?

The case for the Tapestry as a religious work destined for a cathedral is based largely upon external evidence—that is, on comparison with surviving textiles or descriptions of church hangings on both sides of the English Channel. Records show that around 840, Saint Agelme, bishop of Auxerre, France, or-dered for his church a "large number of hangings." Around 985, Abbot Robert commissioned for the Abbey of Saint-Florent of Saumur "dosserets, curtains, and hangings in wool." At the end of the ninth century, Adelaide of Poitou, wife of King Hugh Capet, donated a hanging depicting the terrestrial sphere to the Abbey of Saint-Denis. An Anglo-Saxon woman by the name of Ælfflæd offered a woven hanging (cortinam) to the Church of Ely after the death of her husband, Ealdorman Byrhtnoth, at the Battle of Maldon in 991.[16] The abbot of Saint-Riquier, who died in 1075, took great care to decorate the monastery both "by acquiring cloths and in having hangings made."[17]

That the Bayeux Tapestry was in its earliest mention found among the goods of the Cathedral of Bayeux supports the claim that it was originally intended for a church, as does the unconfirmed observation by the Tapestry's German examiners during World War II that marks could be found on its canvas backing at regular intervals corresponding to the spacing of the cathedral's piers. "No place lends itself better to the lengthy unfurling of this embroidered fabric than the nave of a church, or, better yet, the nave of a cathedral," writes a former curator of the Centre Guillaume le Conquérant in Bayeux.[18] If the Tapestry was made for a cathedral, none would be more likely than that of Bayeux, which was reconsecrated in 1077 by William's brother Odo, who may also have been at the origin of such a large embroidery project.

Though the Tapestry is a great secular public work of art, religious images and acts are spread throughout the story of the difficult succession after the death of Edward the Confessor, the king who would be saint. Harold visits the church at Bosham before departing for the Continent, the hand of God appears over Westminster Abbey as King Edward is buried, Harold's oath is sworn on religious relics, he holds an orb topped by a cross in the scene of coronation next to Archbishop Stigand in the "orans" pose of prayer. The insignia the Normans carried into battle may be the papal banner conferred upon William by Pope Alexander II. Alongside religious images and acts, we see the outer trappings of religion, not only the church at Bosham and Westminster Abbey, but the monastery at Mont-Saint-Michel.

For a work of art created in an intensely religious age, however, the Tapestry, unlike written chronicles, which pay attention to the will of God in human affairs, or *The Song of Roland,* with its repeated "Christians are right, and Pagans are wrong," shows surprisingly little religious reference to 1066. Bishop Odo, the singular religious figure of the Tapestry, may bless the feast before the Battle of Hastings, but he is not a great spiritual figure. A feudal baron with benefit of clergy, he is a "muscular" Christian who participates in the councils of war and leads with William the charge at Hastings. The Tapestry hints at belief not in Christian providence, but in the supernatural, as, for example, in the appearance of Halley's comet and the so-called ghost ships in the margins above and below the spreading of the news of Harold's betrayal. And it contains obscenities that make it more appropriate for hanging in the great hall of a feudal castle than in the Cathedral of Bayeux. Horses sport epic erections as they prepare for battle, a monk touches the head of the mysterious woman Ælfgyva between the scenes of Harold's capture and transfer to William's court, nude women and men cavort with clear erotic intent. All show a concern with the body condemned by the medieval church.

The Tapestry's borders are filled with images of hunting and bear baiting; with real animals, snails, peacocks, camels, lions, birds, and fish; with fantastical animals, griffins, centaurs, and winged beasts; and with animal fables in the tradition of Aesop. This is the very kind of decoration—the drolleries, grotesques, *babouineries,* and *bas-de-page*—found in the margins of many medieval manuscripts. In the twelfth century, the Cistercian Saint Bernard, reacting against what he saw as the laxity of the Cluniac rule, condemned such doodlings as inappropriate to display in a church. "What can justify that array of grotesques in the cloister where the brothers do their reading, a fantastic conglomeration of beauty misbegotten and ugliness transmogrified?" Bernard asks. "What place have obscene monkeys, savage lions, unnatural centaurs, manticores, striped tigers, battling knights, or hunters sounding their horns? . . . One would sooner read the sculptures than the books, and spend the whole day gawking at this wonderland rather than meditating on the law of God."[19]

The Tapestry is a mixed genre. Alongside the high style of defining glorious epic events are the lower-styled animal fables and bawdy tales of the type known to have been recited in the marketplace, at fairs, and after dinner in the great hall of a princely palace. The Tapestry might just as well have hung in such a secular space as in a church.

Gold thread shone
in the wall-hangings, woven scenes
that attracted and held the eye's attention.[20]

Thus the *Beowulf* poet describes the wall decorations of the Scandinavian mead hall, where men from the North drink, carouse, and listen to tales of heroic warriors like Beowulf himself.

Beowulf may belong to the seventh century, but the tradition lasts much longer. In the thirteenth-century Old French heroic poem *Girard de Roussillon,* the guest chamber of one count's palace is "everywhere spread with tapestries and hangings," and other rooms are "so covered around with hangings that you could not see the stone and wood of the walls behind." Both the early-twelfth-century chronicler Orderic Vitalis and the poet Robert Wace claim that "after the death of William the Conqueror, several dishonest servants carried off hangings from his palace at Rouen." Evidence for hangings that not only cover the wall but tell a story is found in a Latin poem from the end of the eleventh or beginning of the twelfth century. Baudri de Bourgueil describes a fabric in the bedroom of William's daughter Adela depicting with inscriptions the events leading up to the Conquest. Certain of the details of Baudri's description—the appearance of a comet, William's council of war, the cutting of forests and building of ships, Harold's manner of death—indicate he has actually seen the Bayeux Tapestry. But details such as the claim that Adela's hanging is made of precious gold, silver, and silk, studded with gems and pearls, make Baudri's sighting of the Tapestry less likely.

Using a one-seventh-scale model, the art historian Richard Brilliant has attempted to arrange the Bayeux Tapestry along the walls of an oblong hall. Placing scene 1 at one corner and important thematic transitions in the corners of the room, Brilliant speculates that the unfinished Tapestry might have ended where it begins, in Westminster Abbey with the coronation of William and a conjectural restoration of some six and a half feet. The Tapestry, hung below the high windows designed to preserve warmth and provide maximum light, would have required a hall 93 feet long and slightly less than 26 feet wide.[21] This is a large room, to be sure, but such dimensions are not incommensurate with the Hall of the Exchequer, the royal castle at Caen, approximately 37 by 100 feet, or the royal hall in Westminster erected before 1100, 67 by 240 feet. The original placement of the Tapestry in a great castle hall would not have eliminated Odo as its patron, for Odo, as the Earl of Kent and the greatest landholder in England after the king, had a predilection for ostentatious goods. He kept palaces on both sides of the Channel and even one in Rome.

It is possible, of course, that the Bayeux Tapestry was intended for what today would be termed "multiuse," that it was transported from castle to cathedral and back and might even have been exhibited out of doors. Despite Saint Bernard's objections, the obscenities in the margins and elsewhere were less of an impediment to hanging in a great medieval church than they would have been after the Reformation and Puritan revolution. Though the events the Tapestry depicts and the cast it gives them may be spectacularly feudal and secular, it is likely that even viewers in a great castle hall would have seen the will of God made manifest in the affairs of men.

Truth to tell, we will never know whether the Bayeux Tapestry was made for cathedral or castle or both. The very need to make it a religious or a secular work is another way of asking whether the Tapestry is an Anglo-Saxon or Norman work of art and is more wrapped up in the nationalistic rivalries of the nineteenth and twentieth centuries than in the original intent and meaning of the object itself. To the extent that the Tapestry is seen as a religious object, originally intended to be hung in a cathedral, it is Norman and French (though Normandy was not reannexed to France until 1203–1204). And to the extent that it is thought to be a secular hanging meant for a palace, it is Anglo-Saxon and English.

On the side of the French, the Conquest was a first crusade, allying as it did the Normans with the pope. One of the justifications of war in Norman eyes was the elimination of Harold's archbishop of Canterbury, Stigand, who had received neither papal blessing nor the pallium in Rome. Though marriage was not yet a sacrament, Harold had married by cohabitation, outside of ecclesiastical purview. His treachery, moreover, consisted in the breaking of an oath, a "sacramentum," which was a sin and fell under church jurisdiction in sacred matters. The proper place to display divine vengeance for Harold's sin was in the house of the Lord.

On the side of the English, the idea of the Conquest as a crusade meant the imposition of Norman popery upon an Anglo-Saxon church uncorrupted by the degeneracy and deceitfulness of Rome. Such an argument became especially acute after 1530 and Henry VIII's break with the Roman church, and it filtered through to the nineteenth century when many English saw the possibility of a return to purer ideals and practices in place in England before the arrival of the Normans and "worldly religion which came in with the Conqueror" (Thomas Arnold, 1846). In such an account, Harold's treachery is no treachery, his sin no sin at all. Rather, he was tricked by William, who held him captive, and any oath he might have sworn was sworn under duress. The Bayeux Tapestry contains the story of a great injustice, but it does not make manifest the divine will in human events. It has, therefore, no place in a church.

· · ·

Who commissioned the Tapestry? Who actually made it?

Dom Bernard de Montfaucon, the Tapestry's "discoverer," claimed William's wife, Mathilda, to be at the origin of a work commemorating her husband's victory at Hastings. This view, based on local legend rather than hard evidence, was no doubt at the root of the Tapestry's change of name in the early nineteenth century from King William's Cloth to the Tapestry of Queen Mathilda. Montfaucon went unchallenged for almost a century. In 1814, Abbé Gervais de La Rue, a cleric in Caen and a gentleman scholar who had spent the decades after the French Revolution in exile in England, maintained that the Tapestry had been commissioned not by Queen Mathilda, William's wife, but by Empress Mathilda, the Conqueror's granddaughter, sometime after 1106, that it had actually been stitched after 1162, and that it remained unfinished at her death in 1167. De La Rue reasoned that the Tapestry could not have survived the fire that destroyed the Bayeux Cathedral in 1106 and that many of the particulars of the story it depicts could have come only from Wace's history of the Dukes of Normandy, the *Roman de Rou,* composed in the 1160s or 1170s.

That Queen Mathilda should be the patron of the Bayeux Tapestry makes it English, stemming as it does from the reputation of Anglo-Saxon women for sophisticated textile work, the so-called *opus anglicanum,* or English work, and from the belief that only women could actually have embroidered it, reflected in the Anglo-Saxon proverb "A woman's place is at her embroidery" ("*fæmne æt hyre bordan geriseth*").[22] And because of records that have survived of wives embroidering hangings to commemorate the heroic deeds of their husbands. In addition to the woven hanging that Ælfflæd offered to the Church of Ely after the death of her husband, Byrhtnoth, we find that in the reign of Cnut, a granddaughter of Byrhtnoth, Ealdswith, received the parish of Coveney in Cambridgeshire from the Abbey of Ely to work on embroidery. King Cnut's second wife, Emma/Ælfgyfu (see p. 120), William the Conqueror's great-aunt, gave to the same Church of Ely "a remarkable '*purpura*' [textile] adorned with gold and precious gems" along with coverings for the altar. Edward the Confessor's wife, Edith, was known for her needlework. William the Conqueror's wife, Mathilda, left a chasuble made by an embroideress called "Alderet's wife" to Winchester Abbey when she died in 1083.[23] William the Conqueror's chaplain and biographer, William of Poitiers, remarks upon the skill of English embroideresses. It is easy to imagine the scene, depicted by the Victorian painter George Elgar Hicks, of Queen Mathilda and her Anglo-Saxon or English ladies embroidering together in one of the numerous workrooms or "ladies' chambers" depicted in Old French literature. Indeed, one of the earliest forms of the lyric is the woman's work song, or the *chanson de toile,* weaving songs whose subject is often a lover or husband absent in the wars.

A little more than a decade after Gervais de La Rue published his implausible ideas about the Tapestry's patron, Frédéric Pluquet, a pharmacist from Bayeux, filled the prescription of his life with the suggestion that the obscenities in the borders eliminated the possibility of women either as patrons or as creators. And in an unpublished lecture delivered to the Mechanics Institute of Lews in 1860, Mark Anthony Lower claimed that "the Tapestry contains some indelicacies deemed incompatible with the idea that a virtuous and dignified lady like Queen Matilda was the originator of the work."[24] Thus began the reign of Odo the patron.

After William, Odo figures more prominently in the Tapestry's version of the Conquest story than anyone else. "I believe that the Tapestry was made for Bishop Odo, and that it was most likely designed by him as an ornament for his newly rebuilt cathedral church of Bayeux," wrote E. A. Freeman, who in 1869 was the foremost authority on the Norman Conquest. Some accept the patronage of Odo but believe he intended it for a palace rather than a church. Others argue in favor of some form of collaboration: Mathilda for presentation to Odo, Odo under Mathilda's direction, Odo for production in Normandy with the financial backing of Mathilda, Odo in Normandy for execution in England by Anglo-Saxon hands, jointly by Mathilda and Odo with the design of a Saxon-Norman artist for embroidery in Normandy by Normans, jointly by Mathilda and Odo with the collaboration of William's other half-brother, Robert of Mortain. Others still maintain that neither Odo nor Mathilda was at the Tapestry's origin, that it was created for the monks of Waltham Abbey, founded by Harold and his burial place. Or that Odo's English vassals Vital, Wadard, and Turold, all of whom are pictured and mentioned by name in the Tapestry, guided its manufacture. The Tapestry is seen alternately as a gift to Odo in return for large landholdings, a defense of Odo after his imprisonment by William in 1082, and a "plea-gift" to William in order to remind him of his brother's crucial role in the expedition and Conquest of 1066.

Where and when was the Tapestry embroidered?

The search for a precise location and date is no less fraught than the quest for a patron. Some scholars maintain with fervor that the Tapestry originated in a French or Continental school, that it was made at the Monastery of Saint-Bertin at Saint-Omer, at Mont-Saint-Michel, or in the Samur region of the Loire Valley.[25] Other scholars claim with equal fervor that the Tapestry was embroidered in England and locate its origins among Anglo-Saxons at Worcester, at Barking Abbey under Abbess Ælfgyva, at Nunnaminster (St. Mary's) in Winchester, or within Odo's orbit in Kent. If in Kent, then Canterbury, England's greatest cultural and religious center, is a likely place for stitching. The Tapestry has been ascribed separately both to Canterbury's cathedral Monastery of Christ Church and to the Abbey of Saint Augustine. Since Odo, Earl of Kent, was never archbishop of Canterbury, the Tapestry might have been made not there, but at one of his estates or one of the Kentish nunneries under his patronage, like Minster-in-Sheppey. Odo would presumably have transported the Tapestry back to Normandy either shortly after it was made or at the time of his release from prison and exile from England by William the Conqueror's son William Rufus.

In almost all understandings of the Tapestry, the question of timing is crucial, and plausible dates for its manufacture vary wildly between the decade immediately following the Conquest, to Gervais de La Rue's suggestion that it was embroidered a century later, to Bolton Corney's claim in 1839 that it was made after 1203–1204 to commemorate the French king's recapture of Normandy, or even after that in order to honor the Bayeux episcopacy of Robert des Ableges (1206–1231), a favorite of the French king Philippe-Auguste. If commissioned by Mathilda, the Tapestry had to have been made before her death in 1083. If commissioned by Odo for Bayeux Cathedral, it would have to be before the reconsecration of 1077. If by Odo for a palace, it could have been made either before his imprisonment in 1082 or between William's deathbed pardon of Odo in 1087 and Odo's death ten years later. If commissioned by Odo's vassals Vital, Wadard, and Turold for the purpose of his defense, the Tapestry was stitched during the period of his imprisonment.

If the Tapestry was sewn in England, it could not have been later than the time of Odo's disgrace; and if in Normandy, it could have been almost anytime after 1066. Speculation about the date of the Tapestry is fed by internal evidence bearing upon the accuracy of its depiction of costumes, hairstyle and beard, arms and armor, heraldic insignias, horses and ships, architecture and decoration, trees, inscriptions, hunting technique, and military strategy as chronological keys to the time it was made. They are the source of much scholarly debate and, in the place of certainty, have brought only further doubt.

In the complete absence of contemporary documentation, we will never know who commissioned the Bayeux Tapestry, Mathilda, Odo, or another. We will never know who actually sewed it, Norman or Anglo-Saxon laywomen or nuns or even monks. We will never know exactly where it was made or when. From our lack of information and uncertainty emerge the most contradictory suppositions rooted in the attempt beginning in the nineteenth century to make it either Anglo-Saxon or Norman—which is to say, either English or French. The Tapestry is, of course, perfect for such speculation. The Battle of Hastings was, in the phrase of a modern critic, "a damn close-run thing." The causes and the outcome of the Conquest are not clear, and either side can read itself into the Tapestry's ambiguities: its mixture of styles, high and low; its showing of King Harold as both untrustworthy and strong, his death the result of a lucky arrow shot and not the wrath of God; its refusal to clarify the nature of Harold's oath or to specify what King Edward said on his deathbed; its ragged right edge, which leaves unresolved the final act of the Tapestry's visual drama.

In the decades following the Napoleonic Wars, heroic poetry and monumental visual works were pressed into the service of expanding nation-states in search of a glorious past by which to build an even more glorious future. And in the long quarrel between England and France, no event was more crucial than the Battle of Hastings, no cultural objects more contested than *The Song of Roland,* sung in the minutes before the fight, and the Tapestry itself.

CHAPTER 3

WAR
BY OTHER
MEANS

IN EARLY JUNE 1833, A TWENTY-FOUR-YEAR-OLD STUDENT
and bohemian, Francisque Michel, wrote a letter to France's minister of public instruction, François Guizot. The move was audacious. Though he still attended lectures occasionally at the Sorbonne, Michel, the poor son of a lycée teacher from Lyon, had failed the entrance exam to the school created in 1821 to prepare students in the science of reading and assessing manuscripts, the École des Chartes. He earned a meager living copying manuscripts at the Royal Library. And now he wrote to request that the government send him to England for the purpose of transcribing unpublished Old French manuscripts in British libraries and museums.

In the three years he had been in Paris, Michel acquired a reputation as an oddball, frequenting the Romantic literary circle of the poet Charles Nodier. There he was spotted by Alexandre Dumas, author of *The Three Musketeers,* who described him as "a digger of old charters, sometimes so preoccupied with his research during the day that he forgets where he is and shows up wearing a Louis XIII style hat and yellow shoes."[1] Dumas's description is telling. In it we catch a glimpse of Michel's nighttime, romantic, heedless, "yellow-shoed" side, which came out in a series of Gothic tales that he composed in the mode of Sir Walter Scott. Yet Dumas also gives a hint of Michel's daytime occupation as a tracker and transcriber of manuscripts. By the time he wrote to Guizot, he had already edited and published six volumes.

Michel was what today would be considered an "independent scholar," paid for duplicating documents in the tradition of the Benedictine monks of Saint-Maur under the Old Regime and continued by the civil authorities after the Revolution of 1789.

Michel was ambitious, tenacious, and bold, part of a new breed of men who, with the arrival of France's bourgeois king Louis-Philippe after the revolution of 1830, sought to free France from the tutelage of the church under the Restoration (1815–1830). The government of Louis-Philippe's July Monarchy rewarded initiative in what was to be a great era of economic and cultural renewal, the beginnings of the Industrial Revolution in a France that had just begun to recover from the upheavals of revolution and the Napoleonic Wars. Michel must have sensed a change afoot, and he was also calculating. He attended Guizot's courses at the Sorbonne before the professor of medieval history was appointed by Louis-Philippe to carry out widespread educational reform. He no doubt met Guizot's chief adviser, Charles Fauriel, either at the Sorbonne or at the Royal Library.

In his daring letter, Michel played on all the themes he knew would fall on receptive ears. He offered to continue in England work already begun in France, to "locate charters and titles, both published and unpublished, for the volume that the Académie des Inscriptions et Belles-Lettres has requested I continue, along with three students of the Royal École des Chartes." Michel emphasized the patriotic value of such a trip. He would bring back from England to France copies of documents that, despite their current location, were part of a French national legacy because they were written in Old French. And he rooted their usefulness in what was seen to be the origin of Anglo-French relations—that is, the Norman Conquest of England. Scholars "cannot study in all its detail the history of the Anglo-Saxon kings and of the Dukes of Normandy," Michel reminded Guizot, without the sources his mission would provide.

Michel's reference to the Conquest reveals a deeper motive. In the proposal that the government send him to England, the wily student set his sights on recovering the original version of a poem sung by a jongleur named Taillefer to the troops of William the Conqueror's army on the morning of October 14, 1066, just before the Battle of Hastings. Others had been on the track of it, but Michel was convinced they were wrong to think that the lost manuscript of the "Romance of Roncevaux" was one of the two recently published poems about Charlemagne from libraries in the Paris region. "Likewise, Sir," he addressed Guizot enticingly, "the mythical history of Charlemagne, . . . the Anglo-Norman poem composed around the middle of the eleventh century on the travels of Charlemagne to Constantinople and the Romance of Roncevaux written in the early years of the first half of the twelfth century, are also to be found only in England."

Francisque Michel could not help thinking of that other letter, the one written in 1828 by Jean-François Champollion, who died only the year before, requesting that he be sent by the government of Charles X to make drawings of Egyptian antiquities. Like Michel, Champollion came from the provinces to Paris before he was twenty. He was precocious and largely self-educated, taught himself ancient languages, and read a paper on the Coptic language to the Academy of Grenoble at the age of sixteen. Most of all, Champollion deciphered the language of the Rosetta Stone, which led not only to a position at the Louvre, but to a chair in Egyptology created for him at the Collège de France. Michel must have calculated that if he could only find the "Romance of Roncevaux," he might dispense with all the exams, the dull courses, and days of copying in the Royal Library. The government might even create for him a position in medieval French literature at the Collège de France. The "Romance of Roncevaux" would be a new Rosetta Stone.

How did Michel know about Taillefer and the "Romance of

Roncevaux," or what would come to be called *The Song of Roland*, without the very sources he proposed to bring back to France?

Roland, Charlemagne's nephew and the hero who died fighting the Saracens in the eighth century, was known as a legend, and a legend bound to national honor. The composer Claude Joseph Rouget de Lisle wrote a poem entitled "Roland at Roncevaux" just two weeks after composing the French national anthem "La Marseillaise" in 1792. Alongside the patriotic "*Allons, enfants de la Patrie*" ("Come, children of the Fatherland"), we find the *Roland* refrain "*Mourons pour la Patrie*" ("Let us die for the Fatherland"). In 1806, with Napoleon at the height of his power after the Battles of Ulm and Austerlitz (1805), the monarchist Claude Auguste Nicolas Dorion published a heroic poem entitled *The Battle of Hastings, or England Conquered*, which features not Anglo-Saxons against Normans, but Englishmen against French. Dorion reminds his readers of the fact, contained in medieval chronicles, that some version of a song about Roland was sung by William's warriors before the Battle of Hastings and that even before that Roland had dipped his sword in English blood. When France invaded Spain in 1823, Victor Hugo, only twenty at the time, assured French soldiers that Roland, the hero who had died in the Pyrenees near the Franco-Spanish border, "looked down approvingly from heaven."[2]

As early as 1814, Charles Nodier, to whose salon Michel would come some fifteen years later, speculated about the survival of an epic connected to Hastings, as did the poet Chateaubriand, who had spent time in England after the Revolution.[3] We know from a review that Michel published in 1832 of a thesis on the "Romance of Roncevaux" that he had read English scholar Thomas Tyrwhitt's 1798 edition of Chaucer's *Canterbury Tales*, in which Tyrwhitt mentions a manuscript without title in Oxford's Bodleian Library, but "which could be an older copy of that which Du Cange cites frequently under the title of the *Roman de Roncevaux*."[4]

Michel knew about Taillefer because of one of the first publications of a work in Old French. In 1827, Frédéric Pluquet, a pharmacist from Bayeux interested in the medieval history of Normandy, published the twelfth-century Robert Wace's *Roman de Rou,* the story of the conquest and settlement of Normandy and England by William's ancestor Rollo up to Wace's own day—that is to say, the reign of William the Conqueror's grandson Henry II (ruled 1154–1189). "Taillefer, who sang very well, was mounted on a horse that raced along, and he went in front of the duke singing of Charlemagne, Roland, and Oliver and the knights who died at Roncevaux" (Wace, v. 8013)—this is a passage that surely must have tantalized Michel. But none of these would have been of much use if Michel had not been alerted to the possibility that the "Romance of Roncevaux" might be in England by a scholarly old priest who worked at the same table as Michel at the Royal Library.

Abbé Gervais de La Rue, born in Caen, Normandy, in 1751, was close to eighty years old by the time he met Michel and the other young transcribers of manuscripts whom he loved to hush when they spoke too loudly or seemed to be stealing a moment of fun from the serious task of transcription. He would tell them of the mythic quality of British museums, claiming to have worked for years at the Tower of London "without ever hearing a peep" from the British scholars working there.

De La Rue had spent a number of years, possibly several decades, in what was the equivalent of forced exile after the Revolution. He had not wasted his time, but used it wisely, reading Old French manuscripts in British libraries as well as presenting a number of papers to the learned societies of England. On February 4, 1796, he read a paper on the poet Wace to the London Society of Antiquaries in which he linked poetry to victory on the field at Hastings: "The minstrel Taillefer, at the head of the Norman army, announced the moment of the celebrated battle of Hastings, by chanting the song of Charlemagne and Roland; and,

*The Abbé Gervais de La Rue, who tipped off Francisque Michel
about* The Song of Roland

FROM THOMAS FROGNALL DIBDIN, *A BIBLIOGRAPHICAL ANTIQUARIAN AND PICTURESQUE TOUR
IN FRANCE AND GERMANY* (LONDON: ROBERT JENNINGS AND JOHN MAJOR, 1829)

repeating this composition, the troops marched on to victory."
De La Rue suggested a connection between Roland and the
Bayeux Tapestry when, in an earlier presentation, a "Letter to the
Earl of Leicester, President of the Society of Antiquaries" read on
December 4, 1794, he wondered whether or not Wace, as "Mon-
sieur Lancelot in his explanation of the tapestry of Queen
Mathilda . . . has contended," knew the embroidered account of
the Norman Conquest.[5] So, too, de La Rue knew that one of the
lines of the Oxford manuscript quoted by Thomas Tyrwhitt

mentions the name "Turold" as the one who either composed or recited the "Romance of Roncevaux"—"Here ends the tale that Turold declines"—and that the Tapestry shows a mysterious dwarfed figure by the name of Turold among the messengers of William the Conqueror to Guy of Ponthieu at the time of Harold's capture. It is more than likely, given the collaboration of the old abbé and the young student in the transcription room of the Royal Library, that it was there Michel learned of an Oxford manuscript connected to Roland.

Upon receipt of Francisque Michel's letter, Minister Guizot consulted his old friend and colleague from the Sorbonne Charles Fauriel, the "father of the renewal of historical studies in nineteenth-century France," whose assessment was favorable but who reminded the minister in a letter written on June 19, 1833, that M. Michel was not one of the independently wealthy scholars of an earlier age: "Not being able to undertake such a trip with his own resources, he needs to be encouraged by the government."[6] Guizot then sent the proposal, mentioning specifically the possibility of learning about the Battle of Hastings and William the Conqueror, to a committee of the Académie des Inscriptions et Belles-Lettres, specialists in Greek, Sanskrit, Arabic, and Chinese, who also approved. Meanwhile, Guizot asked his undersecretary Pierre-Paul Royer-Collard to bring him examples of Michel's published work, not the manuscript editions but anything that might give some indication of the young man's character and political beliefs. Royer-Collard fell upon Michel's review in the *Cabinet de Lecture* of August 14, 1832, of a PhD thesis, *Dissertation sur le Roman de Roncevaux,* that had been defended at the Sorbonne only three weeks earlier. Here, Francisque Michel congratulated "the old University for having, for the first time, given up its Greek and Roman banalities."

Guizot must have thought the young man impertinent, but he must also have recognized that Michel's attack upon the Sorbonne was just the kind of daring that was needed to build a France equal to the great nations of the past. Nor would it have been easy to resist feeling just a tinge of gleeful satisfaction at the barb aimed at the old "Sorbonnards" who had made his life so difficult during the Restoration.

After a personal interview conducted in the early days of July, only a month after receiving the young man's original letter, on July 24, 1833, François Guizot in the name of the July Monarchy granted the modest sum of 1,000 francs to Francisque Michel for the purpose of "a literary voyage to England." Guizot dispatched a letter to Charles Maurice de Talleyrand, the French ambassador to London, recommending M. Francisque Michel, "an educated and energetic young man." Because he was something of a daring freebooter, the minister would keep the scholar on a short leash. He was not at the outset interested in the "Romance of Roncevaux" but ordered, upon Fauriel's recommendation, that Michel be allowed to copy two historical works, the first being Geoffrey Gaimar's *History of the Anglo-Saxon Kings of Great Britain and of the Conquest by William the Conqueror* and the second, Benoît de Saint-Maure's *Chronicle of the Dukes of Normandy*. In addition, regular reports would be required in order to ensure that the transcription of medieval manuscripts justified the expenditure.

As a young Romantic in a Romantic age, Michel must have realized that times were changing, but he could not have known to what extent the arrival of his letter in the Ministry of Public Instruction was a piece of exquisite timing, how well it coincided with Guizot's own ideas concerning the study of national, and particularly secular, history. Guizot was aware that the Ministry of Public Instruction had just recently, in 1828, been separated from the Office of Ecclesiastical Affairs. Indeed, he was one of the professors relieved of their teaching duties in the wake of the religious fervor of the Restoration.

Guizot was aware, too, that the rivalry among France, Germany, and England would be played out in part upon the field of historical and literary studies. The Germans found their national epic *The Nibelungenlied* in the last century, and though Emperor Frederick had scoffed at it at first, hadn't they used this story of the defeat of the Burgundians by the Huns as a rallying cry after Napoleon defeated them in 1806? Guizot knew that in 1819 the Germans had founded a "Society for research and publication of documents related to ancient Germanic history" and had launched a huge publishing venture, the Monumenta Historiae Germanica, aimed at editing sources, especially medieval texts.

An appeal to the medieval past began very early in Germany, with Friedrich von Schlegel, the Brothers Grimm, and the discovery of the folkloric roots of the free tribes of the ancient German forests. And it continued very late, as seen in Himmler's attempt to find in the Bayeux Tapestry evidence of the unity of modern Germans, Anglo-Saxons, and Scandinavians in an original Teutonic race.

In the decades following the Napoleonic Wars, the study of philology, which involved the dating, location, and classification of primary medieval texts, was part and parcel of the construction of empire and of German national identity, aided by the resources of the state and uniting the Academies of Berlin, Munich, and Vienna. The establishment of a chair of Romance philology at the newly captured city of Strasbourg in 1872 was a symptom of the proliferation after 1860 of such posts in a country where study of the Middle Ages represented a catalyst to nationalism and a cultural arm in the wars against England and France.

Guizot knew that the Germans were out to use the Middle Ages to show that Germany had existed for longer than its current political disunity would indicate. He realized that any claim to longevity of this type would end in claims of territorial legitimacy. This is why, on June 27, 1833—that is, between the time of Michel's original request and the government's positive response—Guizot created the Society for the History of France, a private publishing venture by subscription, for the purpose of encouraging "the study and the appreciation of our national history in the context of healthy criticism, and especially through the search for and the use of original documents."[7] At the end of ten years, the Society for the History of France had four hundred members, and at the end of twenty-five years, it had published seventy tomes, many devoted to the Middle Ages. In 1841, the society brought out five volumes of documents relating to the trials—condemnation and rehabilitation—of Joan of Arc, the heroine of another battle in the centuries-old war with the English.

Guizot sensed that the English were not far behind the Germans. The Society of Antiquaries of London had sent the young Charles Stothard to make drawings of the Bayeux Tapestry, which he carried back with him to Britain. With all their antiquarian societies and clubs, the English had begun to publish Anglo-Saxon historical and literary works. The French might have thought the English naïve for having believed initially that their national epic *Beowulf* was written in Danish and not the language of England before the Conquest, Anglo-Saxon, but they published it nonetheless in 1815. That was the same year the English and the Prussians defeated the French at Waterloo. In 1833, *Beowulf* appeared in modern English translation.

Guizot's project of finding and publishing original source texts continued to fulfill the need felt after the Revolution to examine old documents in order to determine ownership, revenues due, and laws. History as a source of law was a venerated feudal principle of the Old Regime in a world in which family memory served as a source of legitimacy and the exercise of rights. But the question now facing the government was how to transform local, seigneurial, and family archives into a national one. The Institute of France had exercised control over archives under the First Empire and the Restoration. But the old specialists in family history were dying out, and February 22, 1821, saw the royal creation of the École des Chartes, a school for the examination of documents, in order to "revive a type of study indispensable to the glory of France."

Just as the kings of the Old Regime had found their history in Greece and Rome, and just as Emperor Napoleon had continued the dream of empire, Guizot and Fauriel together felt the need for a national narrative and for a present in which France might hold its own against Germany and Great Britain. In this, the Middle Ages, as the cradle of French civilization, represented a privileged terrain. However, one would have to find there works dealing not with Greek and Roman heroes, but with French aristocratic ladies and knights and with ordinary citizens, the ancestors of the enterprising merchants, lawyers, and bureaucrats who made up France's "third estate."

Guizot sought to find in the Middle Ages the origins of the French bourgeoisie, "that is to say," he wrote in a letter to King Louis-Philippe on November 27, 1834, "the first institutions which worked to free and to raise the nation."[8] Guizot imagined the rapid construction of a tradition that would embody the new France. In November 1833, the order went out to prefects to seek "documents having to do with our national history" in public libraries and departmental archives. A month later, Guizot submitted an increased budget request of 120,000 francs for fiscal 1835 in order to "accomplish the great task of a general publication of all the important and unedited materials having to do with the history of our country." He had proposed editing himself a thirty-volume *Collection of Documents Relative to the History of France from the Foundation of the French Monarchy up to the Thirteenth Century.* It was Guizot who transformed Versailles into a national museum.

. . .

Francisque Michel arrived in London at the beginning of September 1833 and immediately fell ill. On September 10, he wrote to Guizot complaining of the cost of living in Great Britain. Guizot, as we know from notes written to his undersecretary Royer-Collard, did not want to send more money until he "had seen work already done." The suspicious minister demanded, in addition, a letter from an English physician attesting to Michel's medical condition. But by October 8, Michel had already sent three notebooks of transcriptions and promised ten more each month. On November 8, he wrote to Guizot again protesting a lack of money. He wondered if he might retain the salary earned in France for copying work at the Royal Library in addition to the stipend for copying in British museums, a request Guizot refused. He closed with a reminder that the postage paid by the French government on letters sent to him covered only the route from Paris to Calais and that he had to pay a postage due of 28 francs.

Francisque Michel traveled to England with letters of introduction from Abbé Gervais de La Rue to British scholars, including Francis Douce, keeper of records at the Tower of London. And the English took note even before his arrival. The *Gentleman's Magazine* of August 1833 carried an announcement under the column "Foreign Literary Intelligence" that "M. Francisque Michel has been appointed by the Minister of Public Instruction to go to England, for the purpose of inspecting the public libraries and archives and of making notes or copies of everything he may find elucidating the ancient history and literature of France."

Michel worked assiduously at the British Library, completing the two editions mentioned specifically in the government commission. Guizot's hesitancy subsided, and his enterprising man in London was put on a regular stipend of 500 francs per month. Meanwhile, Michel made trips to libraries in Cambridge, where he met John Mitchell Kemble, who had translated *Beowulf* in 1833, and the acclaimed editor, then still a student, Thomas Wright. There is some evidence that Michel might also have met Alfred, Lord Tennyson, and later he published the first French translation of Tennyson's medieval-inspired *Idylls of the King*.

The event that was to change the face of French letters and even of the nation took place in Oxford's Bodleian Library almost two years after the student's daring letter to the visionary minister. On July 13, 1835, Francisque Michel discovered what he believed to be the poem sung by Taillefer at the Battle of Hastings. "I write to you from the town of Alfred, right near the Bodleian, where I just found ... Guess what?" Michel wrote to his former teacher and patron, Louis-Jean-Nicolas Monmerqué. "The Song of Roland!! It's almost the squaring of the circle" (see insert, figure 2). Monmerqué shared Michel's letter with Guizot. It was from that moment that France knew for the first time the literary version of Charlemagne's expedition to Spain in 778, the attack upon his rear guard by pagans, the death of his beloved nephew Roland, and the emperor's revenge—all of this written in the Old French language at a time when Europe was arguably French.

Michel's enthusiasm stemmed from the knowledge that France had at last found a national epic to rival the English *Beowulf* and the German *Nibelungenlied*. *The Song of Roland* might serve to direct attention away from ancient and distant civilizations, on the one hand, and away from local provincial histories on the other. The old antiquarians like Pluquet and de La Rue had been interested for the most part in the history of Normandy and of Norman families. Pluquet had emphasized in his edition of Wace's *Roman de Rou* its importance for "our Norman history." De La Rue, who had throughout his life lived at the expense of the wealthiest family in Caen, the Mathans, in their Château de Cambes, had promised in his article on Wace that "the genealogist will find many curious and interesting facts relating to ancient families."

Reading the medieval work will, moreover, "furnish any one who may think it worth while to peruse them, with new light upon the history, the government, and the manners and customs of the Normans."

Michel had little use for the Normans, toward whom he at times showed downright antipathy. In his introduction to Benoît de Saint-Maure's *Chronicle of the Dukes of Normandy,* one of the works Guizot had paid for, he describes the bloodthirsty men from the North: "Drawn by the hope of carnage and booty, the Normans, like the bears of their country, swept down from the pole and wanted to take part in the kill; they threw themselves upon the dying, ripped them apart, became intoxicated with their blood; then, satiated, they fell asleep on the breast they had torn apart."[9]

For the French, *The Song of Roland* was a living lesson in patriotism throughout the course of a patriotic century. And if Guizot had been skeptical at first, he was convinced in the end. "The trip of M. Francisque Michel to England," he wrote in his report to the king in December 1835, "has produced significant results," and he mentioned specifically not only the Norman chronicles, but *The Song of Roland.*

Michel was the first to link *Roland* to the Battle of Hastings, and *Roland* became France's *Iliad; Roland* became France. "The essential character of the epic," wrote François Génin on the first page of his 1850 edition of *Roland,* "is greatness joined to naïveté; the virility, the energy of man joined to simplicity, to the innocent grace of a child: it is Homer." Gaston Paris, the son of the man for whom the chair in medieval studies of which Michel dreamed was created in 1853 and who did more for medieval studies in the second half of the nineteenth century than anyone else, urged on the eve of the Franco-Prussian War that the French should "recognize ourselves as the sons of those who died at Roncevaux and of those who avenged them."[10] Around the same time, his colleague

Francisque Michel

PHOTO BY NADAR; © BIBLIOTHÈQUE NATIONAL DE FRANCE

at the Sorbonne Léon Gautier claimed in his 1872 edition of the poem and in clear resonance with the language of the New Testament that *Roland* is "France made flesh" ("*La France faite homme*"). "What we should seek," Gautier prescribed in an 1892 instruction to schoolteachers, "is to read with a vibrating voice and a heart filled with emotion, a translation of our old poem so as to make children admire its simple and profound beauty. We should seize the opportunity of this reading to say to these young Frenchmen: 'Look, my children, how great France already was and how she was loved more than eight centuries ago.' "[11] Paul Lehugeur, lecturing officers at the French military academy in Saint-Cyr, showed how alive the Homeric *Roland* still was in

1900: "*The Song of Roland*," he reminded the general army staff, "is our *Iliad*."[12]

Francisque Michel made many trips to England and Scotland after his discovery of *The Song of Roland* in 1833. Only one, however, was an official government mission. Prosper Mérimée, the author of *Carmen* who was also interested in the archaeology of public monuments and served as senator for life and an adviser to Emperor Napoleon III after 1853, dropped a hint. "You could do a good deed," he goaded Michel, "by publishing something on military equipment. That's a subject that interests the Emperor and with which he is familiar. I advise you to read his book on artillery, which is excellent. . . . Believe me, if you have something new to say, you will attract his attention, but keep in mind, he is not interested in erudition. What he wants is to learn something that he doesn't already know." In 1863, Michel was sent by the French government to England and Scotland for the purpose of retrieving documents connected to the early history of artillery, recently discovered by him "in the archives of Great Britain."[13]

Reacting to the German model of philology, which used the Middle Ages to establish the Germanic roots of France in the Frankish invasions of Gaul and the Germanic roots of England in the Saxon invasions of Britain, both the French and the English pressed the study of medieval documents into national and even military service. Throughout the nineteenth century, the French felt attacked not only by the weapons of war, but by erudition. "With numbers and discipline on their side," wrote the French historian Fustel de Coulanges in 1872, "the German people show in their scholarship the same qualities as in war. . . . German historians form an organized army. . . . One can distinguish the leaders from the soldiers. . . . Each new recruit enlists in the unit of a master, works with him, remains anonymous for a long time like a private, then becames a captain, and twenty new recruits will work for him. . . . They march in rank, in regiments, in companies."[14] Léon Gautier blamed the French defeat of 1870 upon their scholarly defects and the German victory upon their "scientific method": "We face a nation that makes war scientifically, geographically, physically, chemically. For the Prussian fights in the same manner as he criticizes a text, with the same precision and the same method."[15] The historian Gabriel Monod, who served in the ambulance corps in the Ardennes in 1870, sensed that the scholarly gap between Germans and French was due to a "lightness" of national character that rendered French soldiers willfully blind and prevented them from fighting effectively.[16] In a report on the current state of philological studies presented to the Philological Society of London in 1873, the philologist and editor of texts Paul Meyer complained about the disciplined German scholars who invaded French libraries each spring during school vacations "in the hope of finding a topic for a doctoral dissertation."[17]

By the middle of the century, Hippolyte Fourtoul, Louis Napoleon's first minister of education and a specialist in medieval art, issued a decree "encouraging research which, by drawing the attention of experts towards the ancient and glorious traditions of our country, will raise the spirit of national feeling."[18] Fourtoul established a chair in medieval French language at the Collège de France for Paulin Paris, curator of manuscripts of the Royal Library. Paulin Paris concluded his inaugural lesson with the words "Greetings, then, Messieurs, to our Middle Ages . . . greetings to the old national muse." Fourtoul had issued an order in 1856 for the publication of all medieval French literature written before 1328 in sixty volumes of sixty thousand lines each and sent a letter to the scholar in charge of the project, François Guessard, with the exclamation "Publish all, *all,* ALL" handwritten in the margin.[19]

Medieval studies flourished in France after the defeat of the

Franco-Prussian War of 1870–1871. In the four years between 1876 and 1879, the French government endowed 250 new chairs of literature and history, supported by university libraries.[20] Scholars founded journals dedicated to medieval culture: *Revue des Langues Romanes* (1870), *Romania* (1872), *Revue de Philologie Française et Provençale* (1887), *Le Moyen Age* (1888), and *Annales du Midi* (1889). The monuments of Old French literature, many found in English libraries, were edited. With the help of the Rothschild family, the greatest medievalist specialists of their time, Gaston Paris and Paul Meyer, founded the Société des Anciens Textes Français. In the decade after the Franco-Prussian War, there occurred another war alongside the territorial dispute over Alsace and Lorraine: the rush to claim—to locate, copy, and publish—medieval works in Old Provençal, the language of the South, and in Old French.

French national interest in the Middle Ages was matched by a revival of medievalism in England. If the French had their Roland, Charlemagne, and Joan of Arc, the English had their legends of Arthur, Robin Hood, and King Alfred. The English and French fought each other intermittently between the middle of the eighteenth and the first decades of the nineteenth centuries, and genuine military encounters were often continued in the form of cultural warfare. After the English, led by Admiral Edward Hawke, destroyed the French fleet in November 1759, Horace Walpole wrote a poem entitled "On the Destruction of the French Navy," recalling the days of King Arthur. Joseph Wharton's 1761 poem "To His Royal Highness the Duke of York" features Arthur's ghost, which praises those willing to fight the French. At the time of the American Revolution, the poet Edward Thomas invoked Arthurian legend to celebrate Admiral George Rodney's defeat of the French fleet in the Caribbean.[21] In the midst of the Napoleonic Wars, Felicia Dorothea Browne denounced the "iron sceptre" of Napoleonic tyranny with an appeal to "Britannia's heroes," who "live from age to age! . . . From doubtful Arthur, hero of romance, / King of the circled board, the spear, the lance."[22] The Napoleonic Wars culminated in the Battle of Waterloo, where the French were defeated by a combined force of Prussians and English, led by the Duke of Wellington, who was in the aftermath adored as "the new Arthur."

The myth of King Arthur is especially apt, since Arthurian legend was first created in the century after the Norman Conquest. Arthur represented a hero of resistance against the invasion of Britain by the Saxons and a lightning rod of hope that a "once and future king" might return as a liberator from the new oppressors who had come from Norman France. Indeed, for the English the nineteenth century was imagined as a time when England might finally shed "the Norman yoke."

The Scottish novelist Sir Walter Scott may not have invented the idea of Saxon enslavement, but he did much to popularize it in the historical novel *Ivanhoe* (1819).

> *Norman saw on English oak.*
> *On English neck a Norman yoke;*
> *Norman spoon in English dish,*
> *and England ruled as Normans wish;*
> *Blythe world to England never will be more,*
> *Till England's rid of all the four.*

Thus Scott's serf Wamba reminds his Norman oppressors Front-de-Boeuf and De Bracy of an Anglo-Saxon proverb—Wamba, whose neck is literally ringed by a collar showing his servile status: "Wamba, the son of Witless, is the thrall of Cedric of Rotherwood." *Ivanhoe* is set at the end of the twelfth century, yet no one could mistake Sir Walter Scott's reference, in a novel begun just two years after Waterloo, to contemporaneous struggles going all the way back to 1066:

A circumstance which greatly tended to enhance the tyranny of the nobility and the sufferings of the inferior classes arose from the consequences of the Conquest by Duke William of Normandy. Four generations had not sufficed to blend the hostile blood of the Normans and Anglo-Saxons, or to unite, by common language and mutual interests, two hostile races, one of which still felt the elation of triumph, while the other groaned under all the consequences of defeat. The power had been completely placed in the hands of the Norman nobility by the event of the battle of Hastings, and it had been used, as our histories assure us, with no moderate hand.[23]

Scott expresses what was already a current idea in seventeenth- and eighteenth-century political debates—the belief in a golden age when the British "lived as free and equal citizens under representative institutions" before the arrival of a foreign king, his oppressive nobles, and religious policies beholden to the pope.[24] This "Whig" view of history explains, of course, the appeal of King Arthur, the liberator who actually fought the Saxons. It accounts for the British fascination with the legend of Robin Hood, the Saxon hero, as J. Frederick Hodgetts describes him in the children's story *Edwin, the Boy Outlaw* (1887), with "no taint of Norman blood." Early references to Robin Hood date from the second half of the eighteenth century, and the figure of the rebel against harsh Norman forest laws runs throughout the 1900s.

The free, good Anglo-Saxon and the enslaving Norman oppressor is a literary and historical theme sometimes put to surprising use on both sides of the English Channel. The French historian Augustin Thierry, under the influence of *Ivanhoe* and under the received notion that Norman-Saxon relations after the Conquest were the source of contemporary social differences, sided with the freedom-loving Saxons against the "Norman usurpers and imposers of feudalism" in what was a liberal and Republican attack upon the British ruling class. Thomas Carlyle used the Saxon-against-Norman motif as a means of raising the "Condition-of-England Question" and of equating the Saxons with ordinary Englishmen as against the upper classes, though his thinking is perhaps more complicated than that of Scott or Thierry. For Carlyle, both Saxons and Normans are part of the Teutonic race, Normans being Saxons "who had learned to speak French."[25]

In the first volume of his *History of England*, focused upon the period subsequent to the reign of James II, Thomas Macaulay laments that the Conquest "gave up the whole population to the tyranny of the Norman race." Macaulay considers English history, dominated until the end of the twelfth century by kings born in France, to have begun in earnest only with the rebellion against King John and the signing of the Magna Carta of 1215, guaranteeing inalienable rights to the barons of England. In the second half of the nineteenth century, E. A. Freeman made the claim, which historians have echoed ever since, that Edward the Confessor, who had spent eighteen years in exile in France, brought back with him a preference for all things Norman and thus contaminated the "free Teutonic spirit" with "Norman vice." The Normans or the French, Freeman believed, were Catholic, dishonest, and decadent and had disturbed the peace of Europe ever since. Curiously, this is exactly what French historian Jules Michelet thought of the English, which was not without its benefits. It was by hating England, Michelet believed, that France became France.[26]

Though England and France were allies in the Crimean War (1854–1856), that enterprise ended finally in discord between the two. And when it came to the Franco-Prussian War of 1870–1871, many English liberals rejoiced at Prussia's victory over Napoleon Bonaparte's nephew Louis Napoleon, who had fled to London in 1840 after trying to topple the Orleanist monarchy and had returned as emperor in 1848. They saw in Prussia a fellow Germanic people with an enemy in common in the French. "The war on the part of Germany is, in truth, a vigorous setting forth of the historical truth that the Rhine is, and always has been, a German river," E. A. Freeman wrote.

As a Hanoverian, Queen Victoria shared in the Germanic tradition inimical to France. Victoria's mother was the sister of Leopold, Duke of Saxony, and her husband, Albert, was the son of

Statue of Queen Victoria and Prince Albert in Saxon garb

THE ROYAL COLLECTION, © 2006, HER MAJESTY QUEEN ELIZABETH II the Duke of Saxe-Coburg-Gotha. All of their children married either Germans or Scandinavians. Victoria and Albert named their second son Alfred, and no monarch before or after Victoria participated more fully in the tradition of the most celebrated and steadfast Saxon king—Alfred.

> *With grave utterance and majestic mien*
> *She with her eighteen summers filled the Throne*
> *Where Alfred sate: a girl, withal a Queen,*
> *Aloft, alone!*

Thus the poet laureate Alfred Austin, in "England's Darling," read at the diamond jubilee celebration in 1897, commemorated Victoria's coronation. Though she died on January 22, 1901, Victoria's reign was to have culminated in millenary celebrations of Alfred's death in 901. Bishop Creighton of London in *The King Alfred Millenary* claims that the English "might surely feel proud to consider it an absolute fact that our history had gone on since the days of Alfred till now, and that the sign and token of it was that the blood of Alfred still ran in the veins of her most Gracious Majesty Queen Victoria."

The return to Saxon roots was nowhere more evident than in the growth of Anglo-Saxon studies, which worked to establish a connection between the inhabitants of Britain before the Norman Conquest and the British Empire on which the sun never sets. Thomas Arnold, who became Regius Professor of Modern History at Oxford in 1841, just four years after Victoria's coronation, insisted that "we, this great English nation, whose race and language are now overruning the earth from one end of it to the other,—we were born when the white horse of the Saxons had established his dominion from the Tweed to the Tamar. . . . So far our national identity extends, so far history is modern, for it treats of a life which was then, and is not yet extinguished."[27]

Just as the French encouraged the publication of original source texts in Old French, the English sought to make the historical and literary monuments of the Anglo-Saxon world available to a wider public. The antiquarian movement in England spread its interest in old ballads to other works, beginning with the Roxburghe Club, founded in 1812, its members responsible for furnishing reprints of "some rare old tract or composition." The Camden Society was founded in 1838, the Early English Text Society in 1864, with the goal, according to its spearhead, Frederick Furnivall, of a printing "in accessible form of all the English Romances relating to Arthur and his Knights." Furnivall's effort was the culmination of the impetus, begun in the previous century, to claim Arthurian literature as an indigenous British phenomenon rather than simply a translation from the French. In all, some twenty-nine historical societies were founded between 1834 and 1849.[28] Unlike the governments of Germany and France, however, it was not until 1858 that the British leadership became directly involved in publishing works found in state collections, beginning with the Rolls Series.

The publication of Anglo-Saxon works had begun before the arrival of Francisque Michel in London in 1833, yet his hand is to be seen even there. In the report delivered to the minister of public instruction upon his return to France in 1835, Michel mentions that he has compiled along with John Mitchell Kemble "a catalogue of all the works in Anglo-Saxon and in Gothic that I have found in the course of my research." And in the introduction to that catalog, Kemble calls for the English to catch up with the Germans in the science of the study of manuscripts.

The publication of original works was synonymous with an inventory stock of Anglo-Saxon and English as a national tongue. The Reverend Thomas Dale became Britain's first professor of the English language and literature when he was appointed in 1828 to a chair at University College, London. Other universities followed suit. The *Oxford English Dictionary* project, begun in 1842 and not completed until 1920, was more than just a dictionary. It was a virtual inventory—a census—of all the uses of all the words in English from their beginnings to the present. Around the middle of the nineteenth century, the British took stock of their language as a form of cultural property indistinguishable from patriotic sentiment. "The love of our own language, what is it in fact but the love of our country expressing itself in one particular direction?" asked the Victorian philologist Robert Chevenix Trench in 1855.

At its outer limit, the question of linguistic origins became wrapped in race. "The grammar, the blood and soul of the language," claimed Max Müller in a series of lectures delivered at the Royal Institution of London in 1861, "is as pure and unmixed in English as spoken in the British Isles as it was when spoken on the shores of the German ocean by the Angles, Saxons, and Jutes of the continent."

The great conduit of language and literature from the Anglo-Saxons to the English race was Thomas Malory, who was the first, as S. Humphreys Gurteen asserts late in the century, to revive "the good old Saxon" tongue and thus to cast off the Norman linguistic yoke. In Malory, the English found their own. *Le Morte d'Arthur* was the beginning of a process of "reversing the Conquest," in the phrase of Claire Simmons. As the first author of an Arthurian masterpiece, a "master in the telling use of Saxon speech," Malory "took the volumes in existence . . . as a weaver takes his skeins, and, using his pen as his shuttle, wove out of them a history of his 'Round Table,' as Matilda and her maidens pictured the story of the Conquest in the tapestry of Bayeux."[29] Thus, Frederick Dixon uses the metaphor of weaving to express the essential link between the free Anglo-Saxons before the Conquest and Malory, a link completed among the Victorians in what came to be known as the *opus anglicanum,* needlework reviving a much older medieval tradition. "The woman who sews now, sews more beautifully, turning out work more equal to that of her ancestress, the Anglo-Saxon lady," Sir Walter Besant reminds us at the time of Victoria's jubilee in what became a commonplace of the age.[30]

Given the patriotic purpose to which medieval documents and monuments were put, it is no surprise that interest in the Bayeux Tapestry coincided with the growth of rivalry among European states. Almost as soon as the Enlightenment ideals of universal man and common humanity came into being, they were countered by a turning toward medieval history as opposed to the universalizing Greco-Roman past. The Middle Ages were still visible in the French and English countryside in the form of buildings and monuments, whatever their state of ruin. Beginning with the Romantics, the "cult of ruins," and especially old churches, provided what the French poet Chateaubriand termed the "moralization of landscape" in the "midst of scenes of nature," and Victor Hugo, the "vestiges of races past and the sacred bed of a dried river."[31] Alongside the architectural presence of the medieval past, manuscripts were still to be found in church libraries and in castles. As the patriotic study of the Middle Ages grew after 1789, it came to constitute an important element of what made England England and what made France France.

The rivalry between England and France that motivated Francisque Michel to find and publish the actual poem sung on the morning of the Norman Conquest is written into almost all understandings of the Bayeux Tapestry from the time of its discovery until the present—that is, the attempt to determine when, where, by whom, for whom, and for what purpose it was made as a way of determining whether the first Anglo-Norman work of art is English or French. The two most significant scholarly contributions of the end of the last century, which subsume all the rest, participate no less in the will to ascribe the Tapestry to a nation-state. "There is general agreement that it was made in England within a generation of 1066," writes David Bernstein in his extraordinary *Mystery of the Bayeux Tapestry* (1986). Wolfgang Grape refutes Bernstein's conclusions in his equally extraordinary *The Bayeux Tapestry: Monument to a Norman Triumph* (1994): "If we review all the analogies suggested to date, assess the historical evidence and weigh the balance of probability throughout, only one conclusion is possible. The Bayeux Tapestry is a Norman work, probably worked in the 1070s and made in Bayeux."

Whether the Bayeux Tapestry is English or French is much more deeply rooted in the national rivalries of the nineteenth century, setting Germany and England against France, than in the reality of medieval perceptions and events. Extending the famous dictum of Carl von Clausewitz (1780–1831), according to which "war is a continuation of political relations by other means," to read "scholarship is a continuation of war by other means," we understand the attempt to locate the Tapestry's manufacture on one side of the English Channel or the other alongside the publication of founding epic works like *The Song of Roland*, the *Nibelungenlied*, and *Beowulf*, the rise of academic medieval studies, and the uses and abuses of popular literature connected to medieval legends in the complex building of nation-states. In the nationalistic rivalry between Great Britain and France, the Tapestry occupies pride of place.

The Bayeux Tapestry is special, first and foremost, because it is the only one of its kind. There are more than a hundred epic songs extolling the courage in the Crusades and in local skirmishes of the medieval warriors of England and France, but only one pictorial narrative of the great Norman Conquest. Images resembling those of the Tapestry are to be found in other artistic media, sculpture, murals, and manuscripts, but not in large hangings or weavings. The textiles that can be compared to the Tapestry are of a later date.

The Tapestry is also special because, unlike massive archaeological or architectural monuments, it is both prodigious and portable. William may have brought the stones for many of the building projects undertaken in England after the Conquest from the other side of the Channel, but once built, they remained in place. Though one may wonder how the monoliths of Stonehenge might have been hoisted so high, no one argues that they were brought to their present location from somewhere else. Manuscripts, coins, ornamental objects, furniture, textiles, and the Tapestry, of course, are different. They circulated—in trade, in war, in diplomatic and domestic exchange. When Europe woke to the Middle Ages, many were discovered in spots distant from the place of their making.

The movement of cultural objects between the British Isles and France is particularly fluid. Between the Conquest of 1066 and the French recapture of Normandy in 1203–1204, they were one country, and the traffic in goods and artifacts never ceased. Many of the literary and historical documents in Old French are, like *Roland,* still found in British libraries and museums. If the Tapestry was made in England, as many believe, how did it end up in France? How did what began as the unquestionably English King William's Cloth or Queen Mathilda's Tapestry become the French Tapisserie de Bayeux? Was its ultimate destination, as has been suggested, Bishop Odo's palace in Rome, where it would take its place among the great Roman triumphal columns and friezes? The debate over provenance, the Tapestry's status as a religious or a secular object, the question of who commissioned it, and where and when it was actually made are wrapped in national claims, in what was at the time of the Tapestry's discovery a true territorial dispute.

CHAPTER 4

A
STITCH
IN TIME

IN THE LOWER MARGIN OF THE BAYEUX TAPESTRY, AMID THE depiction of one of the shaping events in the history of the West, the Norman Conquest of 1066, lies a scene of everyday life—farmers plowing and sowing a field, harrowing or covering the furrows, another aiming his slingshot at the birds who might eat what has just been sown (panels 21–24). This is the kind of rural sight familiar to country people living on the land or in the villages of southeastern England in the eleventh century, and like so many of the objects and actions of the Tapestry, it points to current custom and event—the first known image in Europe of a horse rather than an ox being used for tilling the soil. We know that the farmers are English because they wear the mustache and mane of hair upon the nape of the neck that throughout the Tapestry distinguishes Anglo-Saxons from the French. The twelfth-century historian William of Malmesbury recounts that a spy caught by William on the eve of the Battle of Hastings and sent back to Harold's camp reported that "almost every man in William's army seemed to be a priest, all their faces including both lips being clean shaven; for the English leave the upper lip, with its unceasing growth of hair, unshorn, which Julius Caesar describes as a national custom of the ancient Britons."[1]

Whoever designed the Tapestry could have seen such a picture in one of the medieval illuminated manuscripts—the calendars, or "labors of the month"—kept in Canterbury, where we

An eleventh-century calendar illumination, month of January

MS. COTT. TIB. B.V. F.3R © BRITISH LIBRARY/HIP/ART RESOURCE, N.Y.

know they were produced and housed before the Conquest and where the embroidered record of the Norman triumph might have been made. Yet the image in the margin is more than merely a scene taken from rural life or the copy of an image found in a book. This particular combination of planting and bird slaying illustrates a story, one of the Aesopian fables known in classical culture and throughout the Middle Ages as "The Swallow and the Linseed." *Aesop's Fables,* originally written in Greek in the sixth century B.C., were translated into Latin in the first century A.D. and from Latin into English by the Anglo-Saxon king Alfred (849–899), who ruled in the last quarter of the ninth. At least this is what the poet Marie de France (ca. 1140–ca. 1190), who translated Alfred's book into French, tells us in her collection of animal tales written about a century after the Conquest. Though Alfred's book has been lost, we can assume that Marie's "Ysopets" and the Bayeux Tapestry must have had a common source, were part of the popular body of such tales that circulated in an age of generalized illiteracy among the few who knew how to write as well as the majority who did not.

The farmers and hunter are actors in the last of the Aesopian fables that limn the edge below the Tapestry's dramatic first act, after such well-known tales as "The Lion, the Buffalo, and the

Wolf," "The Wolf and the Lamb," "The Mouse, the Frog, and the Kite," "The Crow and the Fox," and "The Wolf and the Crane." "The Swallow and the Linseed" is a cautionary tale of men planting flax and of a clever swallow who warns her fellows: "You must know (says the swallow) that all the fowlers' nets and snares are made of hemp, or flax; and that's the seed that he is now a-sowing." Once the flax has taken root, "the swallow told 'em once for all, it was not yet too late." Her warning ignored, the swallow "bids adieu to her old companions in the woods, and so betook herself to a city life, and to the conversation of men." When the flax matures, "it was this swallow's fortune to see several of the very same birds that she had forewarn'd, taken in the nets, made of the very stuff she told them of." Aesop concludes his tale about the relation of causes to effects: "They came at last to be sensible of the folly of slipping their opportunity; but they were lost beyond all redemption first."[2]

"The Swallow and the Linseed" has particular meaning in light of the Tapestry's violent drama of betrayal and death. The artist who undertook to represent the story of Harold's capture and oath, seizure of the English throne, and death at the hands of the man to whom he had broken his word was no doubt attracted by the dog-eat-dog, eat-or-be-eaten, kill-or-be-killed world of Aesop. He was intrigued by the scenario of a wise bird moving away from her foolish fellows and seeking the conversation of the civilized men living in cities. He found irresistible the principle that certain deeds, once set in motion, cannot be undone. Marie de France understood the meaning of "The Swallow and the Linseed" in just this way. In its warning to fools who refuse good advice, the animal tale could easily refer to William and Harold:

> A fool who won't believe the wise
> Who could advise him what to do
> And rescue him from error, too,
> Deserves the painful consequence—
> Now it's too late for penitence.[3]

Yet "The Swallow and the Linseed" is meaningful in another sense, for this tale, which pits the cleverness of the birds against the viciousness of men, turns around flax, the very background material on which the story of the Norman Conquest is embroidered.

The great mystery surrounding the origin of the Bayeux Tapestry is now partially solved by scientific analyses of the physical object itself, yielding answers to the questions of not when, where, or by whom, but of what and how it was sewn.

The Tapestry is made of wool laid upon a background of linen, with a single exception of linen-embroidered thread upon linen in the curious circular object held by one of the ambient figures in panel 107 amid the plunderers after the landing at Hastings and before the final feast. So the answer to the question of how it was made lies in a scene of planting not unlike that of "The Swallow and the Linseed" just under Harold's capture by William's vassal Guy of Ponthieu and the curious dwarfed figure of Turold, who some have speculated is the Tapestry's master maker.

The Tapestry began as fibers of the bast family, which may have been indigenous to the British Isles but more likely came to Britain from the Middle East. The first records of flax as a source of fabric situate it in the alluvial soil of the Caucasus some fifty centuries before 1066. Neolithic man knew flax. Swiss Lake dwellers, the Celtic ancestors of the pre-Roman inhabitants of both England and France, used wool and flax for clothing. The Egyptians knew three or four species of flax indigenous to the region, and from there it spread to Greece, Rome, France, Spain, Holland, Flanders, and the British Isles. The Romans who invaded Britain in the first century A.D. encountered flax, which may have been growing there for almost a thousand years, or since the visits of Phoenician traders anxious for British tin and other raw materials.

The origins of the Bayeux Tapestry lie in the flax plants pulled by their roots—not cut—from the moist soil of southeastern England or western France. The stalks were soaked in warm water and dried in the sun until fermentation and dessication separated the usable inner strands from the chaff of the outer shell. They were then combed with a natural thistle or metal card, spun on a handheld spindle, used since time beyond memory to twist raw fiber into thread, and woven probably on one of the horizontal looms that revolutionized the craft of weaving in the settled cultures of the West. Given the length of certain sections of the Tapestry, the loom might even have had a drumlike roller at one end to wind the threads of the warp and a roller at the other end to receive the bolt of cloth. The cloth was scoured or fulled, then pressed and polished to give a lustrous finished sheen. This would have been one of the new, horizontal, treadle shaft looms that arrived in Western Europe from the Middle East, possibly from as far away as China via Italy or Spain, and that revolutionized the weaver's art. "Men weave with their feet while the women have a stick which moves up and down," wrote Rabbi Rashi of Troyes in the second half of the eleventh century from what would become one of the textile and trading centers on the Continent.[4]

Rashi's observation is important, for what had been throughout the known world and since time immemorial women's work, done in the home while standing up, became in the century of the Conquest also a man's occupation performed sitting down and, eventually, in revived workshops and factories of the type first established in England under Roman occupation. Like Caesar, William the Conqueror was aware of the importance of cloth for military as well as nonmilitary use, bringing with the Norman armies of Conquest textile workers from the Continent to which their ancestors had fled centuries earlier to escape the Saxons. Among all that it portended, 1066 was a watershed event in the making and trading of the raw materials and finished goods that would make England and the Low Countries kings of cloth in centuries to come.

Microscopic analyses done when the Tapestry was removed for cleaning in 1982–1983 show in some detail that the thread of the linen background was turned in a "Z" (counterclockwise) pattern, with a torsion varying between 400 and 460 turns per meter for the warp and 430–650 for the weft, and that the weave of the linen is of a fineness of 18–19 threads per centimeter.[5] The more delicate linen of the Tapestry is folded at its upper and lower edges and mounted upon a coarser linen backing that most certainly was not there from the start. Radiocarbon 14 dating done in the early 1980s situates the backing in a time frame between 1440 and 1680, though current technology would permit a much more precise and narrower temporal window.[6] This 230-foot narrative is stitched upon nine separate lengths of linen, varying between 13.90 meters and 2.43 meters and sewn together so finely that the seams were not discovered before 1874, well after the Tapestry began to attract the interest of connoisseurs and amateur historians.

Before the analyses done in 1982–1983, it was commonly believed that there were eight and not nine sections. We know that the first suture was made after embroidery had been sewn on top of the pieces to be joined. The horizontal mismatching of embroidered stitches upon the linen base lies like an earthquake fault across a road at the top of panels 33 and 34. So, too, the skillful overlappings of subsequent images and writing tell us that joinings after the first were made before the colored wool stitches and fill were sewn upon the linen. In light of the disintegration of the right border, and given what we know about the length of other segments, the Tapestry—by best guess—is missing three to seven feet, at the end of which, it is assumed, there once stood an image of William upon the throne to match that of Harold's coronation after King Edward's death.

If the linen of the background came from the soil, after a long process of transforming flax into cloth, the wool of the embroidery came no doubt from the abundant sheep of Normandy or southern England, such as that shown in the Tapestry in the scene of pillaging after the Norman landing on the coast. Here, too, there is archaeological and written evidence of an increase in the sheep population of England to suggest that William encouraged sheep raising alongside cloth manufacture as a matter of Anglo-Norman governance.[7] The Bayeux Tapestry is in some deep sense a celebration of the textile arts.

Microscopic and chemical analyses tell us that the wool of the Tapestry was degreased, then treated with a mordant containing alum in order to ensure the fastness of the dyes that were applied while the wool was still in the fleece rather than after being spun. Cross sections of individual strands of wool fiber, examined under an electron microscope, show a deep penetration of dye colors, confirming what is visible to the naked eye: The colors of yarn sewn on the surface of linen have faded relatively little compared with the color of the same threads protruding on the other side that have not received nearly the same exposure to light; the threads that have been rubbed and have shed some of their fibers on the outside are no less vividly colored at their core.

Dyeing was an art known to the Romans who had occupied Gaul and England from the first to the fourth centuries A.D. Pliny claims in his *Natural History,* written in the first century, that the Gauls knew how to make "every imaginable color" from the juice of plants. Chromatography of the hundreds of samples of fiber analyzed beginning in 1982 shows ten colors and shades of the original wool yarn of the Bayeux Tapestry: rosy red, darker brick red, mustard yellow, beige or fawn yellow, black blue, dark blue, medium or indigo blue, dark green, medium green, and light green. Physical spectrometry shows traces of luteoline (*Reseda luteola*) and apigenine present in weld, alizarine and purpurine present in madder (*Rubia tinctorum*), indigotin, pastel, or woad (*Isatis tinctoria*), and a lack of the use of tannins.

The colors of the Tapestry, unlike those of subsequent restorations, were produced from natural vegetable dyes and their combination: dyes made from red madder or seaweed, yellow broom or lotus root, and blue woad, which was widely cultivated in Normandy. Three shades of green are a mixture of yellow and blue. Analysis shows that the wool yarn, after dyeing, was spun in an "S" (clockwise) direction with a tension of between 175 and 350 turns per meter and a thickness varying between .6 and 1.8 millimeters. This is hand-spun stuff indeed, and one is tempted to imagine the spinning even in one of the rural dwellings or cottages shown in panels 106 to 108, among the castles, high halls, churches, and cathedral of the Tapestry, in the scene of pillaging between the landing at Pevensey and the Norman feast prior to the Battle of Hastings.

The Bayeux Tapestry is a unique work, and the few scraps of Scandinavian textile wall hangings that have survived, most of which were made after 1066, offer little to guide us as to how an embroidery on linen might have come about. We can only guess on the basis of physical evidence and comparisons with other arts of the period in order to imagine how it might actually have been made. The very size of the undertaking tells us that though it may express the vision of a single mind, it was not the product of a single set of hands. Here the analogy with the cathedral building site, its master architect, masons, craftsmen, laborers, and sculptors working either on-site or in workshops nearby, is apt. The Tapestry contains one such scene of building as a workman in panel 66 places the finishing touch, a weathercock, upon Westminster Abbey, the first Romanesque building in England, completed just two weeks before Edward's death.

William undertook a rebuilding of the parish churches, cathedrals, abbeys, and castles of England after the Conquest that is almost unrivaled in the West, some of it with stone brought all the way from the Continent. The collective work of cathedral building was slow, however, and as an analogy to the making of the Tapestry, nothing like what is suggested in a *Punch* cartoon of July 15, 1966, which shows a harried embroiderer, needle in the air, surrounded by skeins of yarn, stitching furiously as the Battle of Hastings is being fought in the background. The Tapestry probably took more in the vicinity of months or a year than the decades and even generations of a cathedral or great church.

At the end of the nineteenth century, Elizabeth Wardle, wife of silk industrialist Thomas Wardle, enlisted the Leek Embroidery Society of Staffordshire to make a full-scale replica so that England might have a Tapestry of its own. Hers was no local homespun idea, but part of the effort, led by William Morris, to preserve artisanal crafts, including the art of making natural dyes, which had nearly disappeared with the appearance of coal tar– and benzene-based aniline dyes in the 1850s. Thomas Wardle's brother George was the manager of Morris's design firm in London, which assisted in the dyeing of one hundred pounds of wool from the same woad, madder, and weld as those of the Bayeux Tapestry. In a little over a year, thirty-five women completed a reproduction of the Tapestry, which was placed on exhibit in the Reading Museum after touring the United States and Germany. Their task was shortened slightly, however, by the removal, in keeping with Victorian sensibilities, of all traces of male genitalia from the Tapestry's human figures as well as from many of the horses. In the case of the nude figures beneath the figure of Ælfgyva in panel 39 (see p. 119), short pants have been traced over the offending organs, though the trace lines have not been filled with wool stitching.

A closer analogy is to be found in one of the textile workshops of the Middle East, more particularly in the highly organized silk-making factories of Constantinople, whose products were known in the West and to which we will return in the course of our discussion of the Tapestry's overall design and deeper meaning.

A still closer and more immediate analogy lies in the manuscript workshops, or scriptoria, which in the eleventh century would most likely be located in one of the great abbeys or monasteries of England or France. Mont-Saint-Michel, which is pictured in the Tapestry at the mouth of the river Couesnon at the beginning of William and Harold's venture into Brittany, was one of the great centers of manuscript production in an age before the revival of commerce and specialization of labor following the Conquest moved the making of books into more commercialized workshops in larger population centers. William encouraged the making of manuscripts. The man he installed as archbishop of Canterbury, Lanfranc, brought with him from Normandy books and copyists who revolutionized both the hand and the style of English manuscript illumination in the decades following the Conquest. Scollandus, who came from Mont-Saint-Michel to be the first abbot of Saint Augustine's, Canterbury, was originally a scribe. The monastic copy room, or scriptorium, was the end point of the various activities connected to the making of manuscripts, beginning with the preparation—depilation, stretching, polishing, and collating—of parchment, some of the skin possibly from the same sheep that yielded the Tapestry's wool.

In the making of a manuscript, there would be negotiations between the book's patron or purchaser and the master manuscript makers. They would discuss the size and quality of the skins to be purchased, the number and size of illuminations, the richness of the colors to be used (blues made from lapis lazuli were particularly expensive), whether there would be gold or silver leaf, the place and character of marginalia, the quality and luxuriousness of the binding. At the end, a contract might be signed like that between a present-day home owner and builder.

Once agreement had been reached, the master planner in a manuscript workshop assessed the skins in order to fold them in sequential folios that, when cut, would lie flat. So complex, in fact, were the techniques of aligning the first fold with the animal's spine and then folding either twice for a large manuscript (a quarto) or three times for a smaller manuscript (an octo) that the secret of just how it was done was not discovered until the nineteenth century. The master laid out the margins, left and right, upper and lower, pricked the parchment with pins for tethered string, and traced with lead the rulings for writing and the spaces to be left blank. The layout specialist might also suggest subjects and make sketches for illustration. Once the parchment had been laid out and ruled, a reader might read out loud the work to be copied by copyists wielding a quill pen and a pen knife for erasures. A rubricator traced in chapter and section titles, often in the red ink that his name connotes. Using the colors prepared by specialists in the making of ink and paint from some of the same plants that yielded the Tapestry's dyes, illuminators filled in the areas left for images, sometimes laying gold and silver leaf. The same or other artists went to work in the margins, adding the visual glosses and doodlings—the *bas de page* and drolleries that have so puzzled scholars over the years. Binders sewed the carefully folded folios of parchment in a codex book, and, finally, craftsmen made a book cover, some of which were so encrusted with precious metals and gems that they attracted the Viking raiders of monasteries up and down the Seine and along the English and Irish coasts long before the Norsemen settled in what would henceforth become Normandy, the "Land of the Men from the North."

There are many important formal analogies between the Bayeux Tapestry and medieval manuscripts: the horizontal ruling along upper and lower borders filled with meaningful miniatures—Aesopian fables, exotic and domestic animals, floral and geometric decoration, scenes of hunting, bearbaiting, erotica—all along the Tapestry's length, writing to identify people and places amid the main visual tableaux, suturing of the Tapestry's separate sections in what is the equivalent of the binding of a book. The inscriptions that are such an important element of the Tapestry and that serve to identify the people, places, and actions depicted there resemble to some degree the instructions a master manuscript planner would leave on the parchment to guide those who would carry out the visual illustrations. Inspection of the rear of the Tapestry shows that in certain places the inscriptions were sewn before the figures they were meant to identify. Many of the tableaux depicted in the Tapestry, the numerous scenes of council, for example, are so stylized as to lead one to think they must be set pieces from one of the pattern books used by manuscript illuminators in order not to have to reinvent every subject and setting each time. It would be hard to conceive the making of a work of the specific character and size of the Tapestry without something along the lines of the organization that went into the production of a medieval illuminated manuscript.

Again, though we do not know exactly where or when, we know either Queen Mathilda, or Odo, or Odo's vassals conceived of a memorial to the Conquest, to the glory of a husband, brother, or feudal lord. There may have been discussions about the form of such a monument—the advantages of something in stone like Battle Abbey, begun on the site of victory at Hastings almost immediately after the event, versus those of something more portable, the nature of a private rather than a more public work. At some point, one of the advisers to Odo or the queen, like the retainers and counselors pictured in the Tapestry itself, might have mentioned the great victory friezes seen by Anglo-Saxon and Norman visitors to Rome in the course of the tenth century or one of the reports of textile hangings in Byzantine churches brought back by the Scandinavian troops who guarded the emperor in Constantinople.

There would be talk of the materials themselves, whether to use "precious gold, silver, and silk, studded with gems and pearls," as in Baudri de Bourgueil's description of a hanging in William's daughter Adela's bedroom, or whether the embroidered account of 1066 would be made of plainer stuff. The decision to embroider the Tapestry out of wool on linen in all likelihood points to a function, conceived from the outset, that would involve regular unfurling and rerolling, and possibly transport, which would have been rendered more difficult by the interweaving of metal filament and the application of jewels or other ornament. Cost would not have been a consideration, since either Mathilda or Odo had access to the riches for which England was famous at the time of the Conquest. The English complained bitterly about the treasure appropriated from religious institutions and sent to France by Odo after 1066. It remained to find a workshop suitable for such a large-scale venture, though it is also likely that the where of the weaving of the Tapestry was settled from the start and may have influenced the nature of the project.

Somewhere in southern England or western France, in the second half of the eleventh century, at least nine pieces of linen backing along with ten different colors or shades of dyed wool thread, iron needles, shears of a type that had been around since Roman times, design sketches either on loose pieces of parchment or in set-scene pattern books, lead for drawing on linen, and frames for holding cloth stretched and steady were assembled either in a single workroom or in several, either in a religious foundation or in a more secular and domestic hall, for the purpose of embroidering an account of what must have seemed like relatively recent events.

Like any work of art of such a large scale, the Bayeux Tapestry shows an inconsistency or two. In the scene where Guy of Ponthieu speaks to Harold shortly after his capture in panel 20 stands a group of eight men, or at least eight heads, with only eight legs among them. In some of the equestrian figures, the same horse is shown as being of different color. Yet, unlike many medieval manuscripts in which experts in the science of paleography can recognize differences in handwriting that would indicate more than one copyist or painting styles of more than one illuminator, the Tapestry shows a remarkable artistic consistency from beginning to end. Examination of the back of the Tapestry shows a difference in scale and possibly also in skill between, say, the miniaturized scene of Edward's deathbed stacked vertically on top of the scene of his enshrouding, and the rest, and may signal the handiwork of more than one embroiderer. Yet the overall coherence of conception points toward a master artist or designer who imposes his vision throughout. It also indicates that those who actually executed such a single vision must have worked either from a separate drawing or set of drawings or, alternatively, that the pattern for the Tapestry might have been drawn directly upon the linen surface. There is some trace of design marks upon the linen, though these may be related to one or more of the restorations made in the course of its long history.

The nineteenth-century historian Jules Michelet once characterized the Middle Ages as "a thousand years without a bath!" Not so the Bayeux Tapestry, which according to experts has probably been washed a time or two, and such washing, it is conjectured, might have removed sketching in lead or other material beneath the embroidery. Even if the Tapestry's figures had originally been traced directly upon the linen, it is hard to believe that whoever traced them could have worked without some version of a preliminary sketch. An example of drawing on cloth survives from the tenth century in the *Life of Saint Dunstan,* who as a young man had so "developed his skill in the arts of writing, of playing on the lyre, and of painting" that he is called upon by the noblewoman Æthelwynn to draw designs on an ecclesiastical robe to be "embellished with embroidery in gold and precious stones." The cleric is clearly capable of designing inscriptions and other figures within the context of an embroidery workshop and a "team of needlewomen."[8]

So, let us imagine a workroom in which the various textile materials have been assembled, some portion of the linen stretched upon a wooden frame, a set of designs either traced upon the linen or alongside it, and a Tapestry Master who also acts as foreman of a team of embroideresses.

Though those who actually embroidered the Tapestry were most likely women, the designer was probably a man, which tempers somewhat the view of one of the Tapestry's first commentators, Agnes Strickland, that men should not be allowed to speak of the Bayeux Tapestry, since they would "not know how to put in the first stitch."[9] The attribution of the design to a man is based upon an analogy with the male world of manuscripts of this period, as opposed to that of subsequent centuries when women became more actively involved in the making of books. The Tapestry designer was not only possessed of some little clerical training, if only because of the Latin inscriptions, but was also familiar with the dominant art forms of his day—oral and possibly written poetic works such as the fables with which we began and which were used throughout the Middle Ages to teach young boys good grammar as well as good behavior. He might have heard one or more of the heroic poems such as the *The Song of Roland* or the Latin *Song of the Battle of Hastings,* written not long after

the event by Guy of Amiens, uncle of Guy of Ponthieu, who figures in the Tapestry's opening act and actually accompanied
Queen Mathilda from Normandy to England for her coronation
in 1068.

Even with a modicum of education, the Tapestry Master
would have known the Bible, parts of the basic works of the
Church Fathers, books of prayer and psalms, and possibly some
version of either an Anglo-Saxon or Norman chronicle. He
might certainly have come into contact with metalwork, ivories,
textiles in the form of clerical robes, altar coverings or hangings,
other decorative objects, and wood and stone carvings. Of course,
he would have encountered the architecture of either England or
France, or possibly both, as depicted in the Tapestry, though what
is today appreciated as architecture might have seemed at the
time no more than a military stronghold, a town dwelling, a peasant's hut, the palace of a local lord, or God's own house.

The Tapestry Master had a greater knowledge of distant cultures than has heretofore been recognized. He was familiar with
the world of Byzantine silks and knew either directly or by
hearsay of the great victory friezes of the Roman world, Trajan's
or Marcus Aurelius's Column, possibly via a Christianized version commissioned in the early eleventh century at the behest of
Bernward, a monk of Hildesheim, Germany. The Tapestry Master might have seen one of the "Exultet Rolls" of southern Italy,
on which the biblical text was written for a clerical reader alongside illustrations to be shown to the congregation. Though the
Bayeux Tapestry may appear to our eye the work of a naïf, and
though its medium may be that of simple cloth, whoever designed it knew much about the art forms of his day and developed
in his masterpiece, as we shall see, what, at the dawn of what the
historian Marc Bloch calls "the second feudal age," was an international style.

Working either from a sketch alongside or upon the linen, the embroideresses, again with extraordinary consistency, used three basic stitches throughout. The first is a stem stitch, in which the needle comes out of the cloth each time, overlapping slightly the previous stitch in order to form a straight line or a curved line due to the turning of the angle of successive stitches. This stitch can be observed in its simplest state in the Latin inscriptions whose straight parallel, perpendicular, and diagonal lines, sometimes capped with a small serif, resemble the writing of a child who learns to print in capitals. The stem stitch is put to sophisticated use as a tool for sketching. It is used regularly for hands, faces, and unclothed bodies such as the legs stepping into the water as Harold's retinue leaves Bosham or the naked bodies in the margins, as if to imply nakedness via a lack of wool in panels 7, 38, 39, and 123.

The stem stitch suggests fateful consequences in the outline of the "ghost ships" that lie ominously along the lower margin below Halley's comet in panel 75 and the counselor whispering in Harold's ear after his usurpation and when the prospect of invasion is just an idea, stitched or sketched out, and waiting to be filled in. The overlapping joined boards of the ghost ships will reappear in the empty stem stitches of the timber made into lumber in the construction of William's fleet in panel 83. The stem stitch is perfect for the depiction of decorative tiles or stonework on the sides of buildings. It renders the wavy lines of the choppy Channel in Harold's travels to Normandy and back and in William's passage on the night of September 27, 1066, capturing as it does the insubstantiality of water as opposed to the other substances represented in terms of solid mass—the Tapestry's 626 human figures, 202 horses or mules, 55 hounds or dogs, 505 other animals, 41 ships, 37 buildings, and 49 trees.

A variety of the stem stitch, the outline stitch, is characterized by less overlap in its tracing of figures, which are then filled in by "laid and couched" stitches—a laying of wool yarn in a mass that is gathered while another series of threads is stitched at a right angle and the mass secured, or "couched," to give the effect of solidity within the contours of an outline. The outline stitch is to the "couched" colored yarn it contains as the lead surrounding a solid piece of colored glass is to the transparent colors of a medieval stained-glass window. As the yoking of a gathered mass of yarn, giving the impression of little ringlets, the "laid and couched" stitches are perfectly suited for depicting the chain mail of armored knights, the craggy landmass on which rests Mont-Saint-Michel, or the wrinkles in garments. Sometimes, too, the outline penetrates the more solid mass of gathered yarn, as in the case of garments whose folds are represented by internal sketching in yarn of a different color from that of the fill, yielding a certain naturalism of the clothed body.[10]

There is in the Tapestry little attempt at perspective, which is rendered for the most part by the depiction of objects as large and small, as in the larger, closer boats and the smaller, more distant ones shown at the time of William's crossing, or by the use of different-colored yarns, as in the near legs of certain horses sewn in lighter or darker hues meant to give the illusion that the off-legs are farther away. The actual embroidery of the Tapestry must have been astonishingly well prepared in terms of the choice of color. An examination of the bridges of yarn visible from the back shows that the same thread may be used to sew a figure of the main panel, an inscription, and then a border. Such careful planning suggests use of a pattern drawn on the linen and confirms that the different vertical zones of the Tapestry were stitched simultaneously as the sewing progressed from left to right.

So in an account of how—not where, when, or by whom—the Tapestry was made, we might imagine a foot or so a day worked in linear sequence by embroideresses surrounded by baskets of yarn, a ready supply of needles, sketches from the type of pattern books used in the illumination of manuscripts to be followed directly or transferred to the linen, bits of trimmed yarn upon the floor, all under the watchful eye of the Tapestry Master, calculating the length of scenes and the placement of sutures, drawing upon the linen, writing out the inscriptions or spelling them out loud, making suggestions about the decorations in the margins that are less sequential than the events of the main panel, and inspecting the whole at regular intervals.

The Bayeux Tapestry is in some ways like the Torah scroll of the Hebrew scribe, who cannot make mistakes with the impunity of the copyist of a codex book, obliged, in the instance, to recopy only one folio page. Its linen pieces vary between 13.90 and 2.43 meters, and despite the numerous blemishes, repaired tears, and even the waxy substance that has penetrated the linen at certain places, we know from the lack of needle holes that do not seem part of the original design that the Tapestry was more than carefully done. Where such needle holes have appeared, they have, as we know from comparison with drawings made in the eighteenth century, been used as a guide to the restoration of stitches that were there from the start. It is always possible, of course, that major errors were made and that the Tapestry Master simply ordered the imperfect linen strip to be cut off and a new one begun. This might explain the extreme variation in the length of the Tapestry's nine separate linen links. Again, we will never know, since the pieces that remain appear seamlessly joined both by individually embroidered stitches and by theme.

Once the separate sections of the Tapestry were complete, we might imagine a sewing together like the basting sessions of a modern-day quilting bee and possibly a stitching of the whole onto a more substantive backing. As the suturing progresses, the finished linen strips would be rolled upon a winchlike device such as that described by Hudson Gurney, who saw the Tapestry in 1817 "coiled round a machine, like that which lets down buckets to a well," or as sketched in 1829 by the antiquarian Thomas

Frognall Dibdin, who claims that we see the Tapestry rolled in his drawing "precisely as it appears after the person who shews it takes off the cloth with which it is usually covered."[11] (See p. 33).

No matter who actually commissioned the Tapestry or where it was embroidered and assembled, it is hard not to envision regular communication between patron and Tapestry Master, as between Master and embroideresses. If the patron was Mathilda and the work took place in a royal castle, she might have participated on some daily basis in the making; and if it was Odo, he might have received regular reports on the progress of embroidery and even visited the workshop to view, like an architectural building site, the transformation of his idea for a memorial to the Conquest into a woven masterpiece. There might have been a final unfurling and viewing, followed by a first hanging in either palace or church. If in a great castle hall, then celebration of the type described in a medieval romance would have accompanied the Tapestry's "coming out." Musicians might have played and tumblers tumbled, while jongleurs recited a chanson de geste like *The Song of Roland.* It has been suggested that the written inscriptions of the Tapestry are intended as cues to aid the oral poet's memory of significant lyric moments of an epic song, possibly even a lost vernacular "Song of Hastings" alongside Guy of Amiens's Latin *Song of the Battle of Hastings.*[12] If the Tapestry, having been removed from nunnery or castle workshop to a church in either England or France, was first unrolled around the nave of a cathedral, its display might have been accompanied by solemn ceremony and prayers of thanks led by Odo. Odo might in his sermon have recounted the story of the Norman Conquest, turning the historical event in which he participated into the stuff of legend. In either account, the stunning unveiling of the Bayeux Tapestry was only the beginning of its enduring artistic and social effects.

CHAPTER 5

BURIED TREASURE

IN THE SUMMER OF 1937, MRS. EDITH MAY PRETTY, A WIDOW living on her estate in Suffolk, East Anglia, recounted to Vincent Redstone, a local historian and Fellow of the Society of Antiquaries, her dream of the previous night. She had seen "a large white horse with a helmeted rider, then the burial of a man and the flashing of gold objects as they were placed in the grave beside him."

The occasion was the Woodbridge Flower Show, and Mrs. Pretty, known as a lover of the rhododendrons and pine trees surrounding her isolated house on a hill above the river Deben, had heard the rumors. A plowman had found a gold brooch at Sutton in 1835. The *Ipswich Journal* of 1860 reported that a local blacksmith had converted into horseshoes the numerous "iron screw bolts" turned over in a field. An old man with a long folk memory spoke of a fabulous treasure buried beneath the strange mounds of earth visible from her bedroom window. Local farmers reported vague rumblings about grave robbers who had perished long ago. Her nephew came with a dowser's rod and assured her there was gold buried under the largest barrow. Vincent Redstone mentioned the stories about Viking burial mounds in the course of their conversation about the hybrid tea roses that year.

What provoked Mrs. Pretty's dream? Was it the distant memory of a childhood visit to the pyramids of Egypt? She had seen grave digging in the Nile Valley. Was it the diggings of her father, an engineer and amateur archaeologist, who had excavated a Cistercian abbey adjoining their house, Vale Royal, in Cheshire? Was it the loneliness of living with her seven-year-old son after the death of her husband, Colonel Frank Pretty, commander of the Fourth Battalion of the Suffolk Regiment, four years earlier? Was it those trips to London to visit her spiritualist medium, who she hoped would put her in touch with the dead? Was it the coming of the war that gave a sense of urgency to discovering what lay beneath the eighteen tumuli just beyond the garden wall? Edith Pretty had seen the disruptions of war and of human folly even in peacetime. She had served with the French Red Cross at Vitry-le-François and Le Bourget, France, in 1917. She was one of England's first women magistrates.

Vincent Redstone did not hesitate. The very night of the Woodbridge Flower Show, he wrote to his friend Guy Maynard, curator of the Ipswich Corporation Museum. "She has invited me to luncheon to consider the mounds. I suggested that I should bring you with me as having useful experience. Any day but Thursday would suit." Luncheon discussion on Monday, July 26, turned around the exquisite flowers in this year's show, the slight increase recently in visitors to the museum, the deliciousness of the summer strawberries in double cream. Vincent Redstone raised the topic of the mounds. Mrs. Pretty suggested they have a look for themselves. Together they decided to call a local archaeologist to give them sound advice.

Several days later, Basil Brown, who described himself in his diary as having "reliable knowledge of Geography, Geology, and Astronomy," arrived on bicycle, carrying nothing more than a bag of books.[1] A fellow archaeologist describes Basil Brown as "a character: his pointed features gave him the, not inappropriate, appearance of a ferret and were invariably topped with a rather disreputable trilby hat, while a somewhat moist and bubbling pipe protruded dead ahead from his mouth.... He had ... gravitated

to archaeology without any real training thanks to a quite remarkable flair for smelling out antiquities. . . . His method was to locate
a feature and then pursue wherever it led, in doing so becoming
just like a terrier after a rat."[2] Basil Brown agreed to stay in the top
room of Mrs. Pretty's chauffeur's cottage and to direct the digging, assisted by her farmhands, Bert Fuller and Tom Sawyer, for
thirty shillings per week.

The men began digging the first mound but found nothing.

Mrs. Pretty, who watched from her bedroom window, de-
scended the stairs and came out of the house. "Why don't you try
one of the smaller mounds?" she inquired. Whether the suggestion was sheer intuition, triggered by memories of how her father
worked, or the residue of her dream, the results were immediate.
Basil Brown could tell from the different-colored soils that this
was a burial site and, by the raggedness of refill, bits of turf, and
broken pieces of clay and shards of a jug in the "robber trench,"
that he was not the first to dig there. Henry VIII had "dug for
treasure in a mound at Sutton Hough but nothing was found, and
John Dee, the Court Astrologer, was commissioned to search for
treasure along the coast by Queen Elizabeth, and apparently
came to Sutton."[3] Before long, Basil Brown held in his hand
pieces of cremated human and horse bone, an ax head, pottery
shards, and an iron fragment with a domed head at one end and a
square plate at the other. On June 28, 1938, Vincent Redstone arrived with other locals, J. Reid Moir, a tailor of Ipswich turned
paleontologist and chairman of the Ipswich Museum Committee, and Mr. Spencer, museum assistant, both of whom offered
advice about where and how to dig.

Toward the end of summer, Mrs. Pretty observed great excitement among the diggers. Basil Brown held a small rusted object in his hand. "I think that what we have here is part of a ship's
rivet," he said. "A lot has rusted away, but these rivets were much
like a bolt. They would be used to hold the planks of a ship to-

Mrs. Edith May Pretty watching the Sutton Hoo dig on her estate in Suffolk
PHOTO COURTESY OF RUSSELL CARVER

gether." The excitement was tempered by the coming of winter, which made further digging difficult.

Excavation resumed on May 8, 1939. Basil Brown was assisted this year by William Spooner, Mrs. Pretty's gamekeeper, and John Jacobs, her gardener. She hired two constables, P. C. Ling of Sutton and P. C. Grimsey of Melton, to guard the excavation day and night. The diggers found more rivets, aligned every twenty centimeters so as to suggest the joinings of a ship whose wooden hull had rotted away. "We thought it was a Viking ship burial," Brown writes in his diary on Friday, May 13; "Mrs. Pretty seems to be greatly interested," on May 18; "It is now evident that we are up against a far larger thing than anyone suspected," on May 22; "Now we have beaten the record for ships found in burial mounds in the British Isles," on June 2. By the end of the month, Basil Brown had found the other end of the ship, which provisionally measured eighty-three feet. On the evening of Sunday, July 2, he attended a meeting at the Woodbridge Spiritualists' Hall, in the course of which the medium, Mrs. Florence Thompson of London, addressed Brown specifically, describing several people she could not place. "I see green fields which you left for a more important position. Now I see sand, all sand. Someone is holding you up in your business. Assert yourself and go on digging." He reported the results of the "séance" to Mrs. Pretty, who telephoned Reid Moir of the Ipswich Museum to expedite excavation of the ship.[4]

The news of the discovery of a longship ninety feet in length spread as far as the Department of Archaeology at Downing Street, Cambridge. Within days, Charles W. Phillips, Fellow of

Outline of Sutton Hoo longship

Selwyn College, Cambridge, arrived. Astonished at the find, he rang the British Museum and the Government Office of Works. At the end of June, Phillips was put in charge of a new team of professional—academic—archaeologists: Stuart and Peggy Piggott, who cut short their summer painting holiday to arrive on July 19; O. G. S. Crawford, who came to make the photographic record; and W. F. Grimes from the Ordnance Survey. Using "a stout coal-shovel at the end of a long ash handle," penknives, a pastry brush, dustpans, and the bellows from Mrs. Pretty's fireplace to blow off their finds, they continued to dig. On the morning of July 21, 1939, the diggers hit gold—the first piece of jewelry from the dig named after Edith May Pretty's farm: Sutton Hoo.

Before the richest grave in Great Britain, Charles Phillips was heard to mutter, "My godfathers!" and could say nothing but "Oh dear, oh dear" all day. The treasure continued to come—gold ornaments, a buckle, a scepter, a shield, a great silver dish, ten silver bowls, a hammer, a gold purse frame with coins, and a large sword. So great was the find of a single day that when the diggers returned to Bull Hotel, where they were lodged, and Stuart Piggott was asked, "Well, old boy, found any gold today?" Piggott replied, "Oh yes, my pockets are absolutely full." Piggott reports carrying the box "containing the great gold belt buckle in my rather sweaty hand in the pocket of my coat." He met T. D. Kendrick, keeper of British and Medieval Antiquities of the British Museum, at the Woodbridge train station and showed him the buckle in the passenger waiting room. In just seventeen days, 263 objects were brought from the ground. The treasure overflowed the sweet sacks, wooden boxes, and tobacco tins that had been requisitioned to hold them. Mrs. Pretty could not fit the valuables in her safe. She stashed the overflow of objects, buried for thirteen centuries, under her bed. Work was suspended on July 25, Mrs. Pretty would later testify, "as I was giving a sherry party."

The treasure horde of Sutton Hoo had attracted the attention of a British nation on the verge of war. On August 14, 1939, the digging having finished for the year, a treasure trove inquest was held at the Village Hall of Sutton to determine to whom the riches belonged. The jury consisted of eleven residents of Sutton and three of Bromeswell, including a bank official, a blacksmith, a tavern owner, the secretary of the Woodbridge Golf Club, a garbage collector, a grocer, farmers, and a schoolmaster.[5] Officials from the British Museum were present alongside the coroner as the pieces of gold and silver that were not too fragile to travel were exhibited.

Sutton Hoo treasure trove inquest, August 14, 1939

The coroner opened the proceedings by reminding the jury that the custom of treasure trove went back to the thirteenth century: If it could be proven that whoever had buried the treasure had intended to return to claim it, it belonged to the king. If not, it belonged to the owner of the land.

Edith Pretty testified that she had always had an interest in the tumuli on her property; she recounted her conversation with

Mr. Redstone at the Woodbridge Flower Show, her interview with Mr. Maynard of the Ipswich Museum, the employment at her expense of Basil Brown, the men of her estate, and a police guard. C. W. Phillips of Cambridge testified that indeed "the work was done under the control of Mrs. Pretty, who paid all the paid labour." The coroner questioned Professor Phillips about the presence of Merovingian gold coins, about the stones in the jewelry. He read "Exhibit B," Phillips's description of Anglo-Saxon funeral rites: "The custom of burial in a barrow or tumulus is one which has been common in Britain from 2000 B.C. till as late as the seventh century A.D. when the conversion of the inhabitants to Christianity brought it to an end." The effort required for such a burial, the digging of the trench, the hauling of the boat from the river inland, its burial along with precious objects belonging to the dead man, and the public celebrations that accompanied the burial of an Anglo-Saxon chieftain all pointed, Professor Phillips testified, to the public nature of the entombment. Despite the presence of subsequent grave robbers, "there was no intention on the part of those carrying out the burial to recover [the buried objects] later."

The coroner read his statement, concluding that "from the disposition of the precious objects, no less than those of more utilitarian nature and of iron or bronze, it was apparent that the whole deposit was that of the personal belongings of the individual buried in the ship, and intended for his use in the future world." The coroner questioned the archaeologist Stuart Piggott, who despite the lack of a body claimed to have no doubt that "there had been a skeleton there." Then he gave the jury its charge, to find evidence "to justify them in finding that the person who owned the objects 1,300 years ago hid and concealed them with a certain amount of secrecy, and with the intention at some convenient time of resuming possession." It was decided that the Sutton Hoo treasure was not treasure trove and "that

Saxons in Great Britain and that of the Vikings several centuries later, Anglo-Saxon because English archaeologists call it that, the treasure of Sutton Hoo is a global find. The provenance and style of its artifacts range from around the known world—England, the Continent, Scandinavia, and the Middle East. Many of its objects came from the British Isles: a bronze cauldron and iron chain-work like those from Roman Britain; an enameled circular escutcheon with millefiori glass inserts and a large hanging bowl of thin bronze, both identified with Celtic workmanship. The arms from the grave are similar to those found in the burial mounds of Scandinavia: a "ring-sword" made either in Sweden or by Swedish armorers in England, a helmet, and drinking horns. The ship, ninety feet long and fourteen feet wide, is of the Viking type.

Of the coins of the Sutton Hoo horde—thirty-seven small gold coins, three blanks, two small ingots—all were struck on the Continent in the area of France, Belgium, Rhineland, and Switzerland controlled by Merovingian Franks. No two are from the same mint. One coin can be traced to the area of Clermont-Ferrand, northeast France, and the Frankish king Theodebert II (ruled A.D. 595–612). The jewelry—twenty gold pieces, buckles, hinges, clasps, ornamental studs, and strap mounts, containing in all over four thousand garnets—is worked in a cloisonné technique, gold cells upon a gold backing filled in with melted colored glass, practiced in Kent, though originally from the Middle East. The great belt buckle, which weighs nearly a pound, is filled with zoomorphic interlace. The greater alloy of the gold—13 percent versus only 2 percent for the rest of the jewelry—means that it was probably made in England, but, like the purse lid showing a man spread between two beasts, it resembles ornaments from Sweden. The regular lines and cells in "step-pattern cloisonné" of the shoulder clasps, which may derive from Roman parade armor, anticipate the great carpet pages of Hiberno-Saxon illuminated manuscripts from Northumbria of only half a century later.

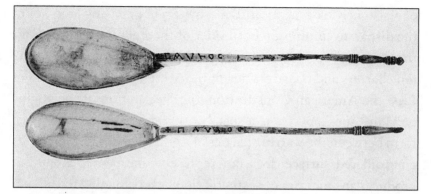

Greek silver spoons from Sutton Hoo inscribed SAULOS *and* PAULOS

Much of the Sutton Hoo treasure traveled to East Anglia from the Middle East: the heavy bronze bowl from Christian or Coptic Egypt; the silver bowls of a Byzantine type; and two spoons, in late classical mold, inlaid in niello, a black paste of silver sulfide, with the names "Saulos" and "Paulos" in Greek characters. A great silver dish 28.5 inches in diameter bears the stamp of the Byzantine emperor Anastasius I (ruled A.D. 491–518) and is thought to have been made on the edges of the empire. Other pieces of silver are from Eastern Europe or the Middle East.

The provenance of the Sutton Hoo hoard makes it less of an Anglo-Saxon than an international discovery and contains an important lesson for the Bayeux Tapestry, which bears on its surface an astonishing mixture of elements from the Scandinavian, Continental, Anglo-Saxon, and Mediterranean worlds. The embroidery is neither Anglo-Saxon nor Norman, neither English nor French. It is not, as has been suggested, purposely ambiguous or a coded message put forth by Anglo-Saxon weavers to undermine the legitimacy of their Norman conquerors. It is not a form of resistance to occupation. The Tapestry is a weaving together of the disparate cultures on both sides of the English Channel after the trauma of 1066, a treaty of peace. Like the monumental written charters and constitutions of the West—the Magna Carta of 1215, the American Constitution, the Declaration of the Rights of Man—the Tapestry is a social contract in written and visual form between the warring parties of a great territorial dispute. Its embroidered surface does not represent one people alone but produces an amalgam of aesthetic elements belonging to the several cultures of the Anglo-Norman world. Its deepest function is to join in a unified work of art contending factions seeking political and social representation both before and after 1066.

Many elements of the Tapestry are clearly marked in cultural terms. Without seeking the original source of a particular design, one can see a resemblance between its embroidered images and objects and those associated with particular parties to 1066—Scandinavian, Anglo-Saxon, Norman, and Continental.

SCANDINAVIAN

Though the Bayeux Tapestry is a unique work of art, it resembles more than any other medieval form the textiles of the Scandinavian world. Among the artifacts and remains discovered by a farmer in a field in Oseberg, Norway, southwest of Oslo, in 1904—a Viking ship, sleds, beds, household utensils, agricultural tools, chests, personal belongings, and the bones of fifteen horses, two bulls, four dogs, and two women—are looms and other implements for weaving, tents, beds, pillows, and a badly damaged piece of cloth that has subsequently been restored. We know that textiles were part of Scandinavian burials from the Arabic description of a funeral by Ibn Fadlán, who visited the Rus or Swedish merchants on the Volga in 922 and reported upon returning to Baghdad, "On the tenth day after the man's death, his ship is hauled ashore to be prepared for the ceremony, a bench covered with carpets of Byzantine silk and cushions is placed on board, and a tent is erected over it."[6] In the funeral pyre around the ship, the body was burned with food, beer, fruits, a dog, two horses, two cows, a cock, a hen, and one of the dead man's female servants or slaves. The grave goods as well as the bones of Oseberg, the richest of the Scandinavian burials, may have belonged to the grandmother of King Harald Fairhair, Queen Åsa, who died in the middle of the tenth century.

Fragment of textile from Oseberg, Norway, buried ca. A.D. *950*
© MUSEUM OF CULTURAL HISTORY, UNIVERSITY OF OSLO, NORWAY

Unlike the Bayeux Tapestry, the Oseberg textile contains no writing and seems to tell no historically specific story. As with the Tapestry, however, its horizontal borders are filled with a geometric chevron design, and the central panel shows a frieze of knights, weapons and shields, birds and swastikas, and horses pulling wheeled chariots with cargo or passengers in procession. The Oseberg textile depicts either the migration of a people or the journey from this world to the next. The horses and chariots resemble Roman models and are themselves draped in places with textiles—cloth within cloth. The headdress, tunics, and triangular pantaloons, wider around the ankles than on top, have the appearance of those found on an Eastern frieze. The figures in profile as well as the overall array of figures in intersecting and overlapping planes evenly disposed across a vertical field so resemble an Egyptian hieroglyphic tableau that one wonders if the hanging buried with Queen Åsa, like the funeral cloths described by Ibn Fadlán, did not come from the Middle East.

A similar fragment of cloth was found in 1867 in the tomb of Haugen at Rolvsøy, Norway. Dating from around A.D. 900, it depicts a scene of five men and two women near a Viking ship.[7] An eleventh- or early-twelfth-century linen, discovered in 1910 in Överhogdal, Sweden, is bordered on all sides by a geometric chevron pattern. Its colored embroidery, filled with animals, some distinctly reindeerlike, features images associated with Old Norse cosmology—Yggdrasil, the world tree, holding together heaven and earth; Odin's eight-legged horse, Sleipnir—alongside Christian symbols, crosses on tops of buildings resembling a church. Like the Bayeux Tapestry, the Oseberg, Rolvsøy, and Överhogdal textiles, *tjells,* or "refills," are woven with colored wools and are long and narrow, indicating that they, too, were intended to be hung around the walls of a home or, after Christianization, in a church. Other examples of Scandinavian textiles—that from Baldishol, Norway, with its mounted knight, and that of Skog, Sweden, with a church and horses—were woven sufficiently after 1066 that the traits they share with the Bayeux Tapestery could be the result of its influence rather than the reverse.

If the Bayeux Tapestry is most like Scandinavian textiles in its material form, its contents are most Scandinavian in the depiction of the sea and especially of boats. The Tapestry is a major source of knowledge about medieval naval archaeology. The vessels of both Harold's crossing from Bosham to Normandy and William's crossing from Normandy to Great Britain are Viking

ships, though Viking sails were square, not curved and triangular.
We know this from Icelandic sagas. King Harald's big ship, like
that of William in panel 98, is lined by a wall of shields atop the
gunwales. "In the words of the poet Thjodolf":

> *The doughty king of Norway*
> *Lined his dragon longship*
> *With a wall of living shields;*
> *No foe could find a gap there.*[8]

The Tapestry's ships are like those on the picture stones of
the Scandinavian world. The eighth- or ninth-century Tjängvide
Stone from Gotland, Sweden, depicts armed warriors standing
on a ship with a square sail, low sweeping hull, and elongated and
soaring stern and prow, as in the Tapestry ships, the whole surrounded by a border of plaits and decorative knots. The eighth-
century Ardre Stone, also from Gotland, Sweden, displays a ship
with a serpentlike figure at both ends; and on the eighth-century
Lärbo Stone, warriors disembark, swords raised, from the dragon
ship to fight the enemy on land. Both images as well as others are
bounded by a braided chain. Braiding of this type is, in fact, an
important feature of the aesthetics of the Scandinavian world
and is sometimes found even on the hull and prow of the boats
themselves. The vessel uncovered in the Oseberg burial mound,
constructed some decades before Queen Åsa's funeral in the
mid–tenth century, is seventy feet three inches long and sixteen
feet nine inches wide. Its beam is limned by a frieze of animals
with a slim midriff and wide rounded shoulders and hindquarters
entwined in a vegetal chain that climbs the high curved prow,
where interlace takes the shape of a spiral, and spiral twists into a
sea serpent. The Viking ship was a "dragon," as they were called in
Icelandic sagas. "The Long Snake" of King Olaf Tryggvason
(ruled 995–1000) was, according to the poet Snorri Sturluson,

Prow of ship buried in Oseberg, Norway, ca. A.D. 950

PHOTO BY EIRIK IRGENS JOHNSEN, © MUSEUM OF CULTURAL HISTORY, UNIVERSITY OF NORWAY

"the best-fitted and the costliest ship ever built in Norway," but King Harald's is a close second: "Above the prow, the dragon / Rears its glowing head; / The bows were bound with gold / After the hull was launched."[9]

THE BAYEUX TAPESTRY

VIT: ·VBE HARO LD: ·VVIDO·PARABO LANT: ·VBI·NVNTII·VVILI

VILLELMI ·DVCIS·VENERVNT·AD·VVIDO NE ·NVN TII·VVILLELMI ·HIC ·VENIT

TVROLD

E·NVNTIVS·AD·VVIL GELMVM·DVCEM ·HIC·WIDO·AD ·DVXIT·HAROLDVM ·AD·VVILGELM·VM· ·NORMANNO RV

RV VM:·DVCEM ·HIC·DVX·VVILGELM:·CVM·HAROLDO·VENIT·AD·PA LATIV SVV

38   39   40   41   42

UBI:UNUS:CLERICUS:ET HIC:WILLELM:DUX:ET EXERCITUS:EIUS:UENERUNT:AD MONTE

ÆLFGY : VA

43   44   45   46

MICHAELIS   ET HIC:TRANSIERUNT:FLUMEN:COSNONIS:ET UENERUNT   AD:DOL:ET:CONAN

HIC:HAROLD:DUX:TRAHEBAT:EOS:

DE ARENA

47   48   49   50   51

N: FUGA:UER   TIT: HIC:MILITES : WILLELM:DUCIS:PUG : NANT:CONTR

REDI : NES

52   53   54   55   56

RA   DINANTES:ET:CUNAN:CLAVES:PO : REXIT: HIC:WILLELM: HIC : WILLELM

DEDIT : HAROLDO:

ARMA

57 58 59 60 61

LLELM VENIT BAGIAS · VBI HAROLD SACRAMENTVM FECIT · HIC HAROLD DVX ·
VVILLELMO DVCI ·

62 63 64 65

REVERSVS EST · AD ANGLICAM TERRAM · ET VENIT AD EDVVARDV · REGE

66 67 68 69 70

REGEM · HIC PORTATVR CORPVS EADWARDI REGIS AD ECCLESIAM SCI
PETRI APLI
HIC EADWARDVS REX
INIECTO ALLOCVTIF IDE IES
HI
ET HIC DEFVNCTVS EST

71 72 73 74 75

IES · HIC DEDERVNT HAROLDO
CORO NA REGIS
HIC RESIDET HAROLD
REX ANGLORVM ·
STIGANT
ARCHIEPS
ISTI MIRANT STELLA
HAROLD

76 77 78 79 80

HIC·NAVIS:ANGLI
CA:VENIT·INTER
WILLELMI:DV RAM
CIS
HIC·WILLELM D
NAVES:EDI

81 82 83 84 85

DVX:IVSSIT
EDIFICARE:
HIC

86 87 88 89

TRAHVNT:NAVES:ADMA RE:—
ISTI
PORTANT:ARMAS:ADNAVES:ET
TRAHVNT:CAR
CVM·VINO:ET AR

90 91 92 93 94

ET·HIC
ARRVM
ARM:IS:
+HIC:WILLELM: DVX IN·MAGNO:NAVIGIO: ET·HIC
MAR E

TRAN···SIVIT ET VENIT AD PEVENE SÆ:

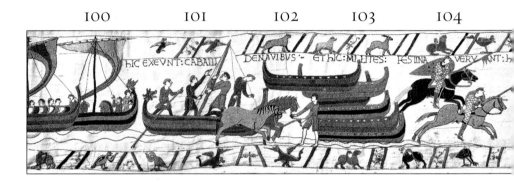

HIC EXEVNT CABALLI DE NAVIBVS· ET HIC MILITES FESTINA VERV NT h

hESTINGA: VT CIBVM RAPERENTVR: HIC EST VVADARD hIC COQVI TVR CARO

ET HIC MINISTRAVERVN MINISTRI hIC FECERVN PRANDIVM ET HIC EPISCOPVS CIBV E POTV BENEDICIT ODO EPS ROTBERT WILLELM

E IVSSIT VT FODERETVR CASTELLVM AT HESTENGA CEASTRA : HIC NVNTIATVM EST WILLELMO DE HAROLD : HIC DOMVS INCENDITVR

VS IN DITVR HIC MILITES EXIERVNT DE HESTENGA : ET VENERVNT

AD PRELIVM CONTRA HAROLDVM REGE : HIC WILLELM DVX INTERROGAT VITAL

AI SIVI DISSET HE EXERCITV ISTE NVNTIAT HAROLDVM
HAROLDI REGE DE EXERCITV
WILLELMI DVCIS

HIC WILLELM: DUX ALLOQUITUR SUIS: MILITIBUS: UT: PREPARARENT SE: VIRILITER

ET SAPIENTER: SE: AD PRELIUM: CONTRA: AN GLORUM

EXERCITU

HIC CECI DERUNT A LEUUIN ET: GYRD: FRATRES HAROLDI RE DI

REGIS · HIC CECI DERVN T SIMVL · ANGLI ET FRA NCI · IN PREL IO ·

HIC ODO EPS BA CVLV TENENS CONFOR HIC EST WILLE DVX BE FRA NCIAC P GRAM

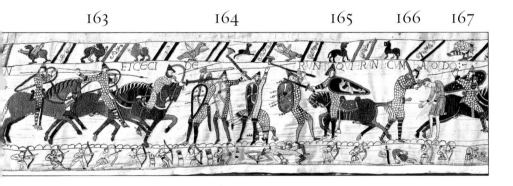

ET CECI DE RVNT AQVI RANT CVM HAROLDO ·

HIC HAROLD REX INTERFEC TVS EST   ET FVGA VERTER

FIGURE I

Cover of *The New Yorker,* July 15, 1944, depicting
the events of World War II.

Original artwork by Rea Irvin. © *Condé Nast Publications.*

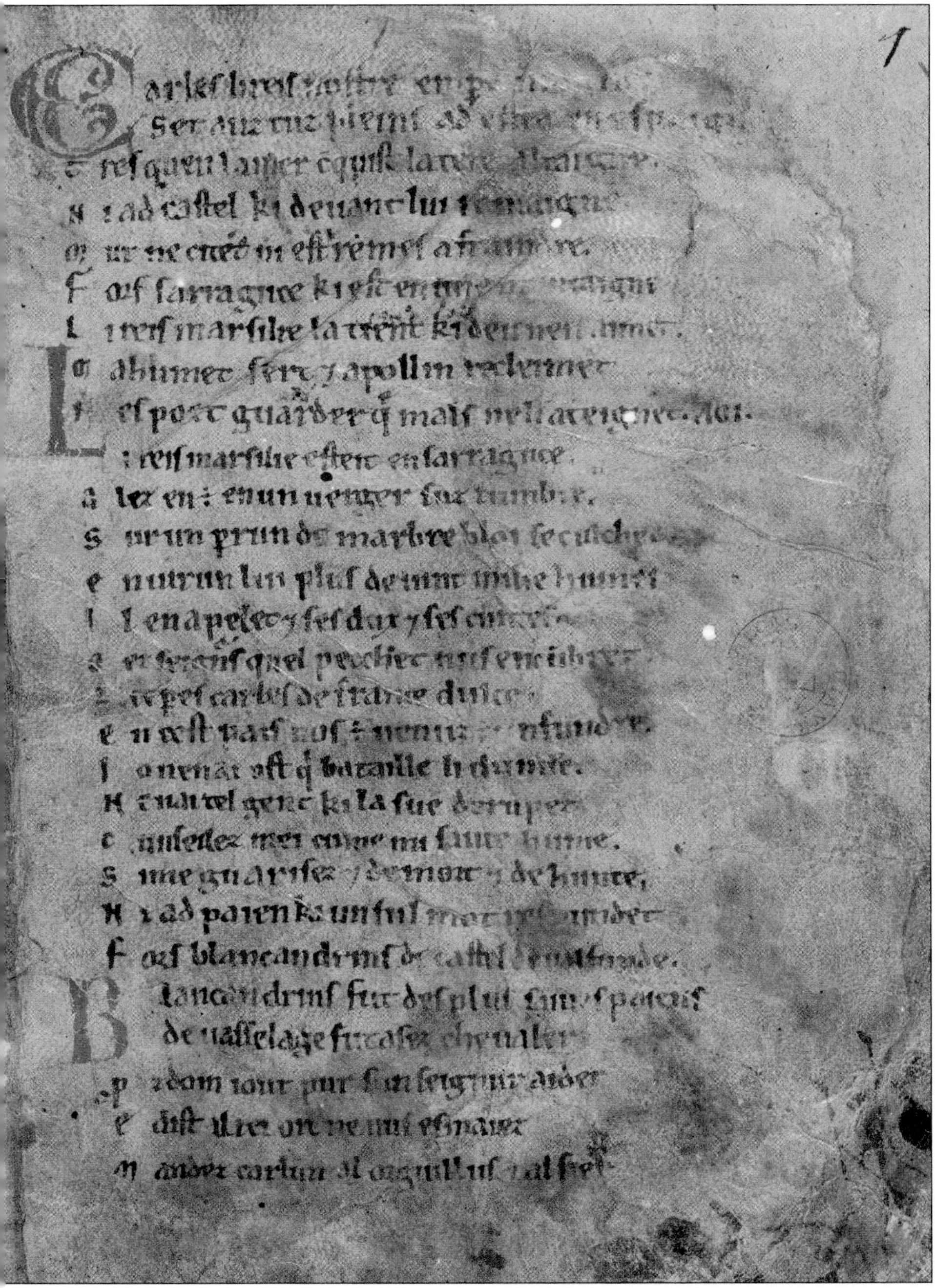

FIGURE 2

First manuscript folio page of *The Song of Roland,* ms. Digby 23, fol. 1r.

© *The Bodleian Library, University of Oxford.*

FIGURE 3

Frontal portrait of Emperor Otto III, 980–1002 A.D.
Munchen, Bayerische Staatsbibliothek, Clm 4453, fol. 24r.

FIGURE 4

Mosaic showing silks in Theodoric's Palace,
Cathedral of Sant'Apollinare Nuovo, sixth century, A.D., Ravenna.

© *Scala/Art Resource, N.Y.*

FIGURE 5
Gunther silk,
showing procession
of Byzantine emperor.
© *Diözesanmuseum,*
Bamberg, Germany.

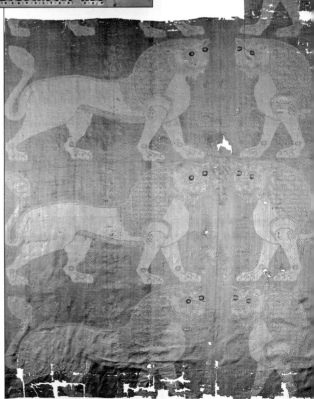

FIGURE 6
Lion silk, c. 976–c. 1025.
© *Diözesanmuseum, Cologne.*

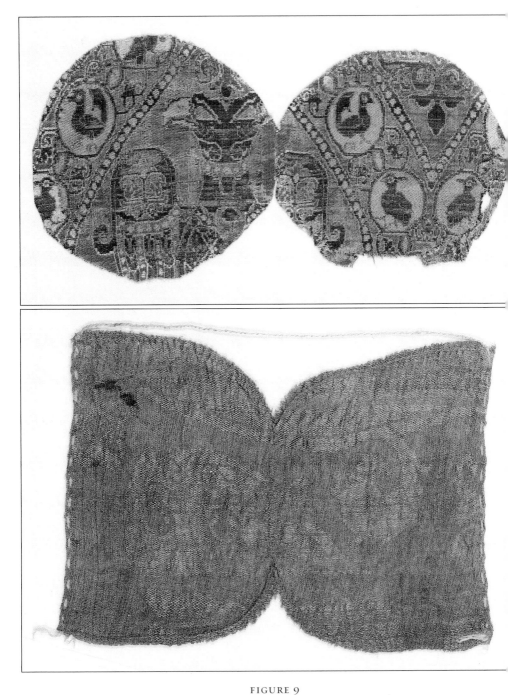

FIGURE 9

Silk sacks, numbers 15 and 32, used to hold seals, Canterbury, eleventh century.

Reproduced with permission from the Dean and Chapter of Canterbury.

The vessels of the Bayeux Tapestry are capped at either end by the knotted dragon heads and beaked sea serpents of the Nordic world. Some of the figureheads on Harold's ships in panels 9–12 are abstract tangles of ornamental wide ribbons, their tendrils miming the waves of the sea, while others assume monstrous human shape. The figures on the prow and stern of William's ships in panels 94–100 are less knotted and more beaked. Both show design elements of the most illustrious Viking artifacts. The interlace of the stern post of Harold's second ship is very like that of the celebrated Jelling Stone of Jutland, Denmark (ca. 965), with its central figure, possibly a religious icon, ringed by interlocking ribbons in the so-called Mammen style associated with the tenth-century iron ax with gold and silver inlay found at Mammen, Jutland, Denmark.

Much of the offensive and defensive arms and armor in the Tapestry is of Scandinavian type, though the close alliance of England with Scandinavia made for a great mixing of weaponry in the Viking age. Both Normans and Anglo-Saxons attack and defend themselves with weapons from the North. Harold's army fights primarily on foot, using the Danish bearded ax. In the first clash in panel 144, the Norman cavalry with couched lance meets the Anglo-Saxon shield wall and axes not unlike those found at Mammen, Denmark, in the Viking camp of Trelleborg, Denmark, as well as in the English digs of the period of Scandinavian occupation. The battle-axes that Harold's men still swing after his death in panel 168 are distinct from the woodman's ax or the carpenter's adze used for the felling of trees and the construction of William's fleet in panel 83, or the adze in the hands of the naked figure in the lower border of panel 38. The swords wielded by both parties to the Battle of Hastings are of the straight, broad-bladed, steel type, the immediate successor of Viking swords found along the estuaries and rivers where they raided, the Vikings having discovered the process for the carbonization of iron to make steel.

The mail garments, or hauberk, loaded onto Norman ships in panel 88 and worn at Hastings are, again, a form of body armor mentioned in sagas from the North as well as in the epics of medieval France. The *Beowulf* poet sings of the "tangled war net," the "ringed mail coat," the "ring-clad lord," the "riveted shirt of mail," and "armour of net-like cunning linked by the smith."

The Bayeux Tapestry was made almost a hundred years before the first use of heraldic emblems as signal devices for the recognition of friend and foe in battle. Yet the twisted-tailed dragons found in the borders of panels 31, 39, 40, 47, 56, 57, 101, and 102; on the shields of William's knights in 15, 26, and 33; on the shield of a Norman with sword striking an Anglo-Saxon with ax in 165; and on the banners of both a fallen and a standing warrior next to arrow-struck Harold are devices of the heraldic type. And they are ascribed by some to the Scandinavian world. Similar dragons are found on the back side of the Jelling Stone as well as among the intricate carvings of the Oseberg excavation—on one of the poles of the sled named after the archaeologist Haakon Shetelig and on the runner of the fourth sled, with its twisted tail, wings, and lip lappet. So, too, the dragons of the Tapestry resemble the animals associated with the Scandinavian Ringerike style, such as that ornamenting a weather vane from Heggen, Norway, or the animals inscribed on rune stones from Stora Ek, and Norra, Åsarp, Västergötland, Sweden. The dragons of the Bayeux Tapestry lack elaborate foliate tendrils, and only the dragon on a Norman shield in panel 165 has the tusks of a true Ringerike beast.

Where the Tapestry is most Scandinavian is not in the depiction of arms and armor, which the Anglo-Saxons shared with the North, but in the peaceful objects of furniture and architectural design that are part of the embroidery's interior space. From the very first panel, the chair in which King Edward sits is built upon legs decorated with the dog's head and feet that are also found on the seat of Guy of Ponthieu in the interview with Harold in panel

20; on William's throne at Rouen in panels 38 and 80; on the chair of the man who seems to be observing earthly events in the border just above Mont-Saint-Michel in panel 43; and on Edward's chair at what may be Westminster Abbey in the scene of conversation with Harold upon his return from France in panel 65. So closely do these details of interior design resemble the animal head-posts from the ship burial at Oseberg, Norway—the "academician's" animal head-post, the "Baroque Master's" head-post, and the "Carolingian master's" head-post—that it is hard not to see them as embroidered renderings of sculptured and decorated everyday objects, bedposts or chair posts—made of wood. The Scandinavian character of the Tapestry's furniture is sustained, moreover, in larger elements of architectural design, if not in the nature of the buildings themselves. The post resting in the water on the seaside building in the scene of Harold's return to Britain in panel 62 is capped by an animal head whose lobelike tendrils may be ears or horns. Horned dragon heads, tongues unfurled, crown the door or gateposts, linked by a decorated upper lintel and wrapped in ascending spirals, between which stands the mysterious figure of Ælfgyva in panel 39.

Finally, a recurrent ornamentalizing tendency characteristic of Norse design lies in the Tapestry's trees. For a work as monumental as the Bayeux Tapestry, made in a world in which people lived closer to nature than in our own, there are remarkably few images of the natural world and nothing on the order of a representation of landscape. On the contrary, the depiction of nature is highly schematic, emblems stitched in outline without the filling-in of laid couch work (see p. 91). The sea is rendered by a series of concentric undulating lines, a hill by the same lines at a sharper angle. Trees, however, are an exception. The tree that stands before Bosham Church in the scene of Harold's arrival from London before embarking for the Continent in panel 4, the tree that grows between Guy of Ponthieu's palace and the emissaries who arrive from Duke William's court in panel 22, and the tree planted before William's throne room upon their return in panel 27 are not sketchy or schematic. Rather, they are elaborately full and stylized, their knotted vegetation filled in, their tendrils ending either in palmettes or in trefoil branches. Strands of undulating interlace lie at the tips of the branches that one art historian, at least, links to "the Ringerike style [of] eleventh-century Norway, Sweden and Denmark."[10] Others, however, maintain that the woven trees found in the Tapestry are closer to the trees and other ornaments found in Anglo-Saxon manuscripts such as the Old English Hexateuch (ca. 1030) currently in the British Library, or the scene of cutting wood from a volume of eleventh-century astronomical treatises, or the initial "D" from a Psalter (ca. 1020) produced at Winchcombe, Gloucestershire, or this calendar illumination for the month of July.

An eleventh-century calendar illumination, month of July

MS. COTT. TIB. B.V. F. 6R. © BRITISH LIBRARY/HIP/ART RESOURCE, N.Y.

ANGLO-SAXON

In all the controversy surrounding the origins and making of the Bayeux Tapestry, of this there can be no doubt: The arts and crafts of Anglo-Saxon England were more highly developed than on the Continent. Stone, ivory, and wood carving, metalwork and jewelry, and especially manuscript illumination flourished under Anglo-Saxon leaders as well as under the Danish kings who ruled England until the Norman Conquest. The Anglo-Saxons and Irish produced the Book of Kells and the Lindisfarne Gospels, the intricacy of whose ornamentation remains unsurpassed. Scholars from the British Isles raised the level of learning at the Monasteries of Fulda and Bobbio. When Charlemagne sought to reform education in the empire he hoped would rival Rome, he sent to England for Alcuin, and when Alcuin arrived at Charlemagne's court, he requested that books be forwarded from home. Alcuin sent for pupils from York "to bring into France the flowers of Britain."

Sculptures and other objects from England of the Anglo-Saxon period share formal elements with the Tapestry. The linear carving from Breedon-on-the-Hill, Midlands (eighth century), shows figures framed in a friezelike series that might have been a narrative. The Franks Casket, with sides inscribed with Old English text in runic signs, portrays scenes difficult to identify but that include the story of Romulus and Remus, the adoration of the Magi, and the sack of Jerusalem by Titus. The Ruthwell, Bewcastle, and Acca's crosses from Northumbria, the Lowther Cross from Westmorland, the Jedburgh Cross from Roxburghshire, and the Easby Cross from Yorkshire all exhibit running plant scrolls, some inhabited by animals, to be compared with the scrolling leaves and animals of the Tapestry's borders. The spiraliforms running along its edges belong to the forms most associated with Anglo-Saxon jewelry, such as the brooches discovered at Pentney, Norfolk, from the second half of the ninth century or the brightly colored millefiori enameled hook escutcheon from the Sutton Hoo hanging bowl.

It is, however, the manuscripts of pre-Conquest Britain that are closest both in form and in content to the Bayeux Tapestry. In a period in which book illumination in Normandy was limited to the floral decoration of initial letters or the filling with figures of "inhabited" initials, Anglo-Saxon book painters saturated the vellum pages of Latin and vernacular works with hundreds of pictures. Canterbury, in particular, was a center of illuminated manuscript production, and several of the books that were known to have been there before the Conquest are of a style and contain images that keenly resemble those of the Bayeux Tapestry: the Harley Psalter, the Ælfric Hexateuch, a copy of Prudentius's *Psychomachia,* and the Saint Augustine Gospels.

The Harley Psalter, a prayer book copied around 1000, takes dozens of pictures from its model, the Utrecht Psalter, which is thought to have been made near Rheims in the middle of the ninth century. Both model and copy show figures finely sketched in ink or colored outline, which are then enhanced with transparent washes or more opaque paint to produce landscape, architectural, and figure drawings that are extremely lively and even give the impression in places of illusionistic space. The Utrecht style of drawing with fill is comparable to the Tapestry's technique of

Scene from the eleventh-century Harley Psalter illustrating Psalm 27:
"Though an host should encamp against me, my heart shall not fear . . .
for in the time of trouble the Lord shall hide me in his pavillion."

BRITISH LIBRARY, MS. 603, F. 15R

embroidery, the stem stitch corresponding to the outline of a drawing, and the laid couch work similar to the enhancing wash or tint between or in and around the lines. Images that may have been taken from the English copy of the Utrecht Psalter include the sower of seeds below panel 22, which is incorporated into the fable "The Swallow and the Linseed" with which we began the previous chapter. Harley 603 also yields a mine of distinctive classical architectural forms, some of which seem to have been integrated into the Tapestry's buildings, such as the circular pavilion with a pedimented façade in panel 25.

The Bayeux Tapestry Master probably knew the Ælfric Hexateuch, named for Abbot Ælfric of Eynsham (955–1020), a major figure in English pre-Conquest culture. This Old English version of the five books of Moses and the book of Joshua from the Old Testament contains some 394 illustrations in various states of completion. Some are framed and independent of one another as well as of the text, while others are linked in series, so as to produce a continuous narrative considered by some to be a precursor of the Tapestry's linear means of telling its story, as in the case of the sacrifice of Isaac. So many figures from the Ælfric Hexateuch reappear in embroidered form that some consider it to have been one of the pattern books used by the Tapestry's designer.

In panel 1, Edward's and Harold's fingers touching in the scene of instruction before Harold's trip to the Continent parallels the scene of Joseph giving instructions to his steward in the Ælfric Hexateuch. The man with a slingshot in the border beneath panel 23, another image incorporated into "The Swallow and the Linseed," resembles that of Abraham as bird slinger. Conan II's escape by rope in the course of William and Harold's siege of the town of Dol at the end of the Breton campaign looks very much like the escape of one of the spies from Jericho in the book of Joshua; even the bricks of the town walls are similar. Edward's reception of Harold upon his return from Normandy in panel 64 seems to reproduce Isaac's blessing of Jacob, right down to the length of the seated Edward's fingers. The long necks of the standing figures can also be found in the "wrung necks" associated with the Winchester style of illumination, as in the example of the evangelist Luke from the Judith of Flanders Gospels in New York's Morgan Library. The carpenter wielding an adze in the scene of boat building for William's fleet in panel 84 is a dead ringer for the Ælfric Hexateuch Noah with whom he shares shoulders and beard.

Other images from the Tapestry trace their provenance to Anglo-Saxon manuscript illuminations. In the scene of plundering along the English coast in panel 107, the curious figure holding what looks like a coil of rope—which contains the only piece of embroidered linen thread among the wool of the Tapestry—is so close to the figure of Labor in the late-tenth-century manuscript of Prudentius's *Psychomachia* that we must assume either that the Tapestry maker was inspired by this copy of a late classical work or that there was a common source. Finally, much has been made of

*An eleventh-century Anglo-Saxon Bible illustration
of Abraham driving away the fowls*

BRITISH LIBRARY, COTT. CLAUDIUS B, IV, F. 26V

the scene of Norman feasting before the Battle of Hastings in panel 112 as a reproduction of a manuscript image of the Last Supper and possibly the version contained in the Saint Augustine Gospels, which shows a round table, with Odo in the seat of Christ.

The Bayeux Tapestry is a multimedia work with images and writing, and the forms of the Latin inscriptions running its length like sub- and supertitles belong, according to some linguists, to the Anglo-Saxon world. The abbreviation "7" for "*et*" is in the period used more readily in the manuscripts copied in Great Britain than in those of the Continent. Certain spellings, especially those connected to people and places, are characteristic of Anglo-Saxon copyists. The AT HESTENGA CEASTRA in panel 116, for example, using AT for "*ad*" and CEASTRA for "castellum," looks like an insular form. The same is true for the name of Edward the Confessor,

Miniature of the Last Supper, St. Augustine Gospels, Canterbury

CORPUS CHRISTI COLLEGE MS. 286, F. 125R; COURTESY OF THE MASTER AND FELLOWS OF CORPUS CHRISTI COLLEGE, CAMBRIDGE

which appears twice as EADWARDUS. The "William" of the Conqueror appears in different spellings, three times in the Normanized form of WILGELM—using the intervocalic G to approximate the French Y-sound, as in BAGIAS for "Bayeux"—compared with fifteen instances of WILLELM current in Anglo-Saxon texts. The most convincing philological evidence of Anglo-Saxon script, however, lies in the Old Danish personal name of Harold's brother GYRÐ (panel 151), the Earl of East Anglia. Only an English-speaking clerk could have spelled Gyrth with a barred Ð, a form of the runic letter *thorn,* for TH.

The name ÆLFGYVA, alas.

Between the dragon head-posts and lintel of panel 39 stands a woman below the inscription UBI CLERICUS ET ÆLFGYVA—

"Here a clerk and Ælfgyva." The cleric's arm extends within the frame to touch her head. A naked figure crouches in the border below.

One of the great mysteries of the Bayeux Tapestry, Ælfgyva has been identified as an abbess installed by William the Conqueror at Barking; Harold's sister involved in an unhappy love affair with a clerk from Rouen; Edith, daughter of Count Ælgar, sister of Counts Edwin and Morcar, the widow of Griffith, king of the Welsh, to whom Harold is married; Eadgifu, the former abbess of Leominster, who was the lover of Sweyn Godwineson, Harold's elder brother and possibly the mother of Hakon, who went with him to Normandy in the early 1050s and was released in 1064; William's great-aunt Queen Emma/Ælfgyfu, whose first husband was the Anglo-Saxon king Æthelred, with whom she had King Edward the Confessor, and who, it is rumored, passed off the newborn child of a priest as the son and heir born of her second husband, King Cnut; and, finally, William's wife, Mathilda, and possibly the patron of the Tapestry, compelled by modesty to "use the adopted name of Ælfgyva."

Amid the myriad identifications of Ælfgyva as well as the scandal surrounding both her image in the Tapestry and her historical reputation, one thing, and one thing alone, is certain. The name Ælfgyva—sometimes written Ælfgyfu—is of Anglo-Saxon origin. Witness Emma, the sister of William's grandfather Duke Richard of Normandy, who changed her name to Ælfgyfu when she married the Anglo-Saxon king Æthelred.

NORMAN AND CONTINENTAL

When it comes to elements of the Tapestry identifiable with Normans, the evidence is very slim; this despite the fact that its subject and conception relate a great Norman victory. The name "Turold" above the dwarfed figure holding the horses of William's emissaries to Guy of Ponthieu in panels 23–24 was a name common in eleventh-century Normandy. Turold is one of only three figures of the Tapestry singled out by name and who are not identifiable historical personages. And like Ælfgyva, Turold has elicited a certain amount of controversy ever since Agnes Strickland in the 1840s claimed that the Tapestry was "designed for Matilda by Turold, a dwarf artist, who, moved by a natural desire of claiming his share in the celebrity which he foresaw would attach to the work, has cunningly introduced his own effigies and name, thus authenticating the Norman tradition, that he was the person who illuminated the canvas with the proper outlines and colours."[11] Others have identified the Turold of the Tapestry as the Turold who became abbot of Peterborough after the Conquest; as Turold who was chaplain to William II; as Turold of Brémoy, bishop of Bayeux in the twelfth century; and as the Turold mentioned at the end of *The Song of Roland* and who has in turn been recognized as the poet, the scribe, or the performer of France's first epic. Along with Wadard, who in panel 107 guards the provisions of the Norman troops, and the scout Vital, who in panel 128 reports to William, a Turold of Rochester was known to be a vassal of Odo and to have held land in Kent.

Some of the buildings of the Tapestry have been ascribed to specific Norman sites and architectural types, both in overall structure and in detail. William is represented in panel 37 at his ducal seat in Rouen, an original Norman palace if ever there was one, though the building shown is a vague combination of generic features belonging to Tapestry buildings on both sides of the Channel. On their way to Brittany, William and Harold pass by Mont-Saint-Michel, an authentically Norman monastery, despite its location at the western perimeter of the duchy near the border of Brittany. The warriors lay siege to three strongholds of the Norman motte-and-bailey type at Rennes, Dol, and Dinan, schematically represented wooden structures atop an earthworks mound; and this is just the type of defense the Normans construct in panel 116 after landing on the English coast.

The earliest example of Romanesque architecture in England—Westminster Abbey, where Edward is buried in panel 67—is considered to have been inspired by such Norman buildings as the main abbey church at Jumièges, rebuilt between 1040 and 1067. One of the characteristics of Norman design, the chevron pattern found on the edges of capitals and arches of Romanesque churches, appears as a series of diagonal bars separating the animals and other figures along the Tapestry's upper and lower borders. William wears a garment covered by such zigzags as he rides past Mont-Saint-Michel in panel 42. The zigzag reappears within the diagonal bars beneath William, who observes Harold taking his oath, beneath Harold accepting the crown, and in the space beneath the Norman feast and war council.

Though the zigzag or chevron is characteristic of Norman and of Romanesque design, its origins stretch much farther east than England or France, to the Middle East, as can be seen in a fragment of marble cornice beneath the dome of the north church of the monastery at Constantine Lips, Constantinople, constructed in A.D. 907. The alternating diagonal bands inhabited by plants and palmettes along with the accosted birds, in this case peacocks reminiscent of the Roman world, recall the edges of the Bayeux Tapestry, which contain many elements from antiquity and especially classical animal fables. The fable "The Swallow and the Linseed" is only one of the Aesopian tales to be found in the borders. These distant travelers hark back to Aesop the slave and Greece of the sixth century B.C., whence they made their way to Rome and to Western Europe via adaptations and translations in the first century A.D. and Latin copies known widely in the medieval West.

The fables in the margins of the Bayeux Tapestry have been interpreted in a variety of ways—as having a purely decorative function and little relation to the central narrative; as constituting a running commentary on specific main panels and thereby eluci-dating the character and motivation of the drama's main protag-onists; as relating less to the central narrative than to one another; as being a moralization of Harold's betrayal; and as being a satire of the Norman point of view from the English side and thus a form of immediate resistance to invasion. Yet amid the scholarly disagreement, one thing is clear—that the Tapestry fa-bles, which have traditionally served as a mirror of princes, a guide to noble behavior, and a warning to those who behave ig-nobly, are of particular relevance to the Tapestry's central story of succession, alliance, oaths taken, betrayal, and revenge. They turn around reversals of fortune, issues of royal justice and privilege, right reason, and ambition.

In "The Mouse and the Frog," in the lower border of panel 11, a frog, anxious to swallow a mouse, tries to drown it by attaching a string to its foot and plunging into deep water until both are swept away by an observant kite, which ignores the mouse and devours the frog instead. Here the moral is very simple, and in an Old French version of the fable from the second half of the twelfth century, Marie de France, the first woman writer of the Anglo-Norman world, insists upon the logic of the Golden Rule. Marie's rendering has particular significance for the Bayeux Tap-estry, for she claims to have translated her Aesopian tale from the English book of the Anglo-Saxon king Alfred; and even if this is not true, it is likely that Marie and the Tapestry Master were working from a common source.

> *With cunning villains this is clear:*
> *They never will have friends so dear*
> *That they, in honour of their friend,*
> *Could bear a single penny spend.*
> *Without compunction, they are glad*

If they can trick their good comrade.
And yet it happens every day:
Those folk who torment in this way
And think that others they'll ensnare, will
Find that they place themselves in peril. (v. 83)[12]

What would the medieval viewer of the Tapestry familiar with the popular animal tale have taken from "The Mouse and the Frog"? He or she might have thought in the first instance of Harold as a "cunning villain" who placed himself "in peril." Or the wider story of the Conquest, which we will take up in our next chapter, might have come to mind. That is, the attempt by Harold's brother Tostig, allied with the Norwegian king Harald Hardråda, to capture England just two weeks before the Battle of Hastings and William the Kite's swooping down to seize the land that both Harald and Harold contested.

"The Wolf King," in lower border panel 10, recounts the tribulations of the lion king's withdrawal from the world. In council, the animals request "that he provide another lion." Yet, the lion "answered that he had no heir."

And thus it was they chose the wolf,
For no one else was bold enough
To dare take anyone but him
(Though all thought wolf a villain grim).

The lion agrees to the appointment of a wolf as his successor under the condition that the new king take an oath not to eat meat.

But when he had been bound by oath,
And when the lion had set out,
Such craving wolf had for meat
That he made plans to use deceit. (v. 37)

This is a fable that could not have failed to resonate with the dramatic crux of the Bayeux Tapestry, the childless Edward the Confessor's impending death, the struggle for succession, oaths, deceit, and both Harold's and William's ambitions, their cravings for meat.

Hunting is one of the obsessive themes in the Bayeux Tapestry, which contains, after all, a consuming great manhunt in William's slaying of Harold, who is depicted consistently ready to hunt and was known historically as a skillful hunter. Harold leaves his initial council with Edward in panel 3 with a falcon on his arm, as hunting dogs give chase to rabbits. The falcon is still on his arm as Harold boards ship in panel 7, and dogs, perhaps those seen running in panel 14, are carried aboard. Harold is captured by Guy of Ponthieu as soon as he makes landfall, and together they ride toward Beaurain, each with a falcon on his arm. Harold and Guy arrive at William's palace with falcons and hunting dogs still in tow in panel 34. Nor is hunting as a theme limited to the main panels. It figures prominently in the lower borders: in the bird slayer of "The Swallow and the Linseed" under panel 23, and in the chase beneath panel 27, which is of special significance. It occurs as the messengers arrive at William's court to announce Harold's capture, and the hunter with horn and hounds moving from left to right is met head-on by a hunter with a stick and hounds coming from the opposite direction. This is one of the few instances in the Tapestry in which action moves from right to left. The juxtaposition of hunters moving toward each other leaves the stag, caught in the middle like Harold in William's custody, in the position of a cornered beast.

The scene of human hunters is preceded in the lower border of panels 15–16 by a fable known in the Middle Ages as "The Lion, the Buffalo, and the Wolf," in which the animals of the hunting party track and kill a deer. When the time comes to share the spoils of the chase, the lion claims the kill, which has been divided into four parts, to be entirely his. The first part, he argues, is his rightful portion as king; the second part comes to him as a member of the hunting party; the third is his "by right because he killed the deer"; and the fourth belongs to him, the lion threatens, "because anyone who took it would be his mortal enemy."

In "The Wolf and the Lamb" of the lower border of panel 7, a lamb, accused by a wolf of drinking upstream from him, points out that in reality he is downstream ("my water comes from you"); to the accusation that his father did the same six months prior, the lamb argues logically that he was not born yet—all of which serves only to precipitate violent attack, as language gives way to animal instinct or appetite:

> *"So what?" the wolf responded next.*
> *. . . The wolf then grabbed the lamb so small,*
> *Chomped through his neck, extinguished all.*

Several Aesopian fables appear more than once. "The Crow and the Fox," which is featured in the lower borders of panels 6 and 40 and in the upper margin of panel 63, contains the well-known story of a crow with a piece of cheese in its mouth and a clever fox who flatters the crow into singing, thus causing the cheese to drop into the fox's possession. Though most versions end with the fox running off with the cheese, the Tapestry designer adds a third image of this tale made famous in the seventeenth century by Jean de La Fontaine, by showing in the upper edge of panel 63 the cheese back in the mouth of the crow. Thus, we might understand that William is the crow, Harold the fox, and the cheese the kingdom, all in consonance with Edward's known designation of William as his heir, Harold's brief seizure of the crown, and William's ultimate recovery of what originally was his. The reversals of the tale are rendered by the artist as a reversal of physical positions relative to each other, which is particularly significant in fables that are about being on the bottom and coming out on top. In its initial rendering in the border below panel 6, the crow is on the left and the fox on the right, yet in the border above panel 63, the crow is on the right and the fox on the left. "The Fox and the Crow" summons up the great replacement in the post-Conquest world of Saxons by Normans in the holding of the cheese/land, of which William's own half-brother Bishop Odo of Bayeux offers such a stunning example when he became Earl of Kent and the greatest landholder in England after the king.

"The Wolf and the Crane," which appears in the lower border of panel 9 and the upper border of panel 62, shows a similar reversal of figures and of fortune. A wolf that has a bone stuck in its throat summons a council of animals for help, and when none seems apt, the crane volunteers:

> Her neck was long, her beak was great;
> With these, the bone she'd extricate.
> The wolf promises a "grand reward
> If he were cured, his health restored."

But when the crane has performed the service of which only it was capable, the wolf breaks his promise:

> "Already her reward she has!
> When she into my throat was poking.
> I might have cut her off by choking."

"The Wolf and the Crane," which, like "The Fox and the Crow," appears above and below Harold's departure to and return from the Continent, turns around deceit, opportunism, and a turning of fortunes translated into shifting positions vis-à-vis each other. In the rendering in the border beneath panel 9, the crane is on

the left and the wolf on the right, yet they end up in just the opposite relative location in the margin above panel 62. Interest-
ingly, too, the reversal is also graphic, for the repetition of both
"The Fox and the Crow" and "The Wolf and the Crane" occurs
precisely where it is written HIC HAROLD DUX REVERSUS EST AD
ANGLICAM TERRAM ("Here Duke Harold returned to En-
gland"), the Latin past participle of *reverto, revertere* signaling both
a return and a turning around of fortune. While the Norman
crane can refer only to the captured Harold, whose head, while he
was in Normandy, was literally in the mouth of William the wolf,
the English crane refers to William, whose head, upon Harold's
return, is about to enter the mouth of Harold the wolf when he
usurps the crown that William considered to be legitimately his.

The image of that usurpation came to the Tapestry from Continental sources and stands as a unique moment within a work of
art that is both long in physical extension and long in temporal
duration, covering as it does some two to two and a half years
from the time of Harold's trip to Normandy until his death at
Hastings. The scene of Harold's coronation in panel 72 contains
the only image in the Tapestry's 230 feet of figures looking directly at the viewer. Archbishop Stigand faces forward in the em-
blematic pose of prayer such as can be found in works like an
eleventh-century image of Saint Clement from the lower basilica
of San Clemente in Rome.

While the great majority of the Tapestry's 626 human figures
are shown in strict profile with only half a face and one eye showing, and a few are shown in some version of three-quarter view
with a face partially averted, Harold upon the throne is shown
frontally. Seated and crowned, Harold holds what is not quite a
scepter, but a rod, or "virga," in one hand and an orb topped by a
cross in the other; his feet, set at an angle oblique to each other,

rest upon a raised pedestal; his robe is draped in a "V damp fold"; the figure is contained, as in many of the Tapestry's interiors, by what seems like a constructed architectural frame. These are the attributes of imperial power from Rome and Byzantium to Jean-Auguste-Dominique Ingres's portrait of Napoleon painted in 1806.

The full face is one of the ways of representing both spiritual and worldly sovereignty passed from late antiquity to the Middle Ages. Frontal Harold in majesty surely had its predecessors in the portraits of the evangelists and Christ in majesty found in the ancient Italian style, in the portrait of Saint Luke from the Evangelary of Saint Augustine (sixth century); in an illumination from the eighth-century Irish Gospels of Saint Chad; or in an image from the "Poem of Caedmon," which originated with Bede in the seventh century and was supposedly translated by King Alfred in the ninth. The depiction of kingship in this last image is in many ways closest to the Bayeux Tapestry not only because of the royal pose, but because of the odd calculation of heads and limbs attached to the seven men standing next to the king on only five feet. The five men standing to the right of Harold in majesty in panel 73 share eight feet among them.

The most obvious predecessors of frontal Harold, and the means by which earlier images of kingship passed to the Tapestry Master, are the imperial Carolingian portraits such as the image from the year 846 of Charles the Bald, grandson of Charlemagne, with scepter and orb with a cross painted upon it. The reign of Charlemagne, or the Carolingian Renaissance, is associated with the dream of Roman revival, and the ambition is preserved in the portraits of emperors long after Charlemagne's death in 814 and long after the dream of imperial unity had devolved into chaos. The Ottonian or Germanic emperors of the tenth century preserved the frontal system of representing sovereignty, as can be seen in a portrait of Otto II, with scepter and orb with cross in

his hands and feet upon a pedestal, all contained with an artifi-
cially constructed architectural space, from the region of Trèves
of around 985; or in the manuscript illumination of Otto III,
emperor from 983 to 1002, from Reichenau of 998 (see insert,
figure 3). The Bamberg Apocalypse, probably also made at Reichenau around 1001, shows the frontal Otto III with scepter and
orb being crowned by Saints Peter and Paul.

The embroidered portrait of King Harold in majesty, in the
tradition of the emperors of centuries past, puts him on a plane
different from every other of the Tapestry's figures, which are in
profile. The faces in profile, which include both horses and men,
appear as if they are two-dimensional. In their alignment along
the plane of action, the face and figure in profile are inscribed in
time and move in the direction of history. They are oriented and
point to a narrative climax at the Battle of Hastings. The same is
true of the less frequent figures shown in three-quarter view
whose two eyes we can see, though unlike Harold they do not
look back. On the contrary, their eyes seem to be looking at some
other person, object, or activity along the Tapestry's horizontal
scenic plane. Taking only such faces nearest frontal Harold, what
is surely the three-quarter Odo in panel 80 receives the order
from William to construct the Norman fleet; the woodsman in
panel 83 looks attentively at his coping ax; one of the three-
quarter carpenters in the upper part of panel 84 appears to be
handing something to his co-worker, while one of the carpenters
in the lower portion of 84 works assiduously on the gunwales of a
boat. The full face of Odo in the feasting just before battle in
panel 112 casts its glance upon the others at table or the servants,
but his visual field does not penetrate beyond the bounds of the
Tapestry. Unlike Harold in majesty, Odo does not look back.

In looking back at the viewer, Harold assumes the full measure of kingly power. The image of the frontal saint, Christ, or
emperor shares in the uncanny visual phenomenon of painted or

embroidered or sculpted eyes that seem to be looking at the viewer, that appear even to follow the viewer, who moves from side to side relative to the fixed portrait that we know to be unmoving and inanimate. The frontal eyes come alive, and what they see is no less than everything. They are all-seeing and omniscient in keeping with a depiction of imperial power as omnipotent. Harold in majesty is all-powerful because he is depicted as in the line of emperors and kings painted in this way and because no one and nothing escapes his gaze. He is for a brief moment in the Tapestry's long and tightly woven narrative outside of history and time. Like the true ruler, he has only one role: to see and to be seen. His being, abstracted from becoming, renders visually the assumption that things are as they seem and will always be as they are. The appearance of Halley's comet in the upper border of the next scene and the ghost ships in the border below, however, are sure signs that time is suspended only temporarily and that history is about to return to reclaim its own.

Why would the Tapestry Master have included a picture of imperial Harold in a narrative intended to commemorate the Norman Conquest and ending with Harold's ignominious death?

Harold in majesty is an integral part of the Tapestry's deepest function—that is, to unify the contending parties to the shock of Hastings and to the territorial dispute that continued to shake England long after 1066. William may have vanquished Harold upon the battlefield, but subduing the whole of England, as we shall see in our conclusion, took considerably longer. The residue of resentment and bitterness among the Anglo-Saxon population—the "Norman yoke"—persisted, as we saw in chapter 3, well into the nineteenth century, when it shaped early understandings of the Tapestry. The depiction of Harold in majesty does not necessarily make the Bayeux Tapestry an Anglo-Saxon creation, nor does it place its maker on the side of the English. Along with the demonstration of Harold's physical strength in pulling men out of the treacherous river Couesnon in panel 45, it gives the Anglo-Saxon party its due by showing Harold, who was, after all, the most powerful man in England with the exception of William, as a king in the line of kings. Frontal Harold is part of the Tapestry's aesthetic and strategic weaving of the inhabitants of Anglo-Normandy into a people.

Harold in majesty gives the strongest indication of how the damaged Tapestry might have ended were it not in shreds in the aftermath of Harold's death and the flight of the English. If the Tapestry still possessed the seven feet thought to be missing at the end, there is little doubt that we would have seen an image of William in majesty to counterbalance that of Harold as the last in the line of omniscient and powerful imperial frontal faces. William's last look would have been the last word.

Some of the objects and images of the Tapestry identified with Scandinavian, Anglo-Saxon, Norman, and Continental culture were themselves mixed even before the Conquest. The elements most truly Scandinavian or Anglo-Saxon turn out to be either a blend of both or, as we shall see, something else altogether. It would be surprising for things to be otherwise, since English and Scandinavians were in contact in the British Isles under the more or less constant domination of Danish and Norwegian leaders from the ninth to the mid–eleventh century. The difference be-tween a Viking and an Anglo-Saxon longship can be a hard call for the trained archaeologist. The figures on the prows and sterns of Viking ships are similar to the golden beaks on the ships of the Anglo-Saxon kings—Æthelstan, Cnut, and Hardecnut. Harold Godwineson presented to King Edward a ship with a golden lion at the stern and a golden-winged dragon at the prow. In Caed-mon's verse paraphrase of Genesis as well as in the Ælfric Hexa-teuch, both produced in eleventh-century Canterbury, Noah's

Ark is figured as a Viking ship with a dragon prow very much like those of the Tapestry.

The resemblance between Viking and Anglo-Saxon dragon-headed prows is striking, and both recall the use of animal heads to eject Greek fire from the fronts of boats of the Byzantine world, which visitors and mercenaries from Scandinavia might have encountered well before the Norman Conquest. Anna Comnena (1093–1153), daughter of Emperor Alexius I (ruled 1081–1118), recounts in the memoir she wrote about her father that "from time to time he used to board a ship . . . and give advice to the ship-wrights about their construction. . . . On the prow of each vessel he had the heads of lions and other land animals affixed; they were made of bronze or iron, and the mouths were open; the thin layer of gold with which they were covered made the very sight of them terrifying. The [Greek] fire to be hurled at the enemy through tubes was made to issue from the mouths of these figure-heads in such a way that they appeared to be belching out the fire."[13]

An eleventh-century Anglo-Saxon Bible illustration of Noah in the Ark

MS. COTT. CLAUDIUS B. IV, F. 14R. © BRITISH LIBRARY/HIP/ART RESOURCE, N.Y.

The arms of the men from the North were indistinguishable from the arms of the British Isles, as there were Swedish armorers working in England, and swords, shields, and helmets captured in battle were often reused. A helmet found at Coppergate, York, inscribed with the Old English name "Oshere," is decorated with lappet-lipped animals that degenerate into plant scrolls resembling the decorated objects of the Oseberg, Norway, ship burial. The chain mail depicted in the Tapestry is identical to the "tangled war nets" from Scandinavian digs or to the mail incised upon a stone frieze from Old Minster, Winchester. An eleventh-century carving in Saint Paul's church yard, London, is as fine an example of the Scandinavian Ringerike style as the beast etched on a bronze weather vane from Heggen, Norway, of the same period. The Scandinavian dragon on Norman and English shields may be the Dragon of Wessex, Harold's emblem, stretched upon a standard in panel 168; both are similar to the wyvern, or winged dragons, in sculpture of the Midlands, as in the Easby Cross, Yorkshire. The shield dragons of the Bayeux Tapestry are similar to that on the shield excavated at Sutton Hoo. And startling as it might seem, nothing resembles the shield dragons of the Bayeux Tapestry so much as metal pieces from the Middle East such as a door knocker from southeast Anatolia currently in the Berlin Museum of Islamic Art.

Whether the mixing of elements from the Scandinavian, Anglo-Saxon, and Norman worlds occurred before or after the Tapestry was embroidered is of little consequence. The overall purpose and effect of such a blending lies in the desire for unity among the peoples to whom such elements might have once, if ever, originally belonged before, as a people, they became entwined.

Such a peaceful vision of the making of what had to be a collective artistic undertaking works implicitly in favor of the Norman conquerors who had the most to gain from the peaceful reconciliation of parties in the decades after 1066. But this does not make the Tapestry a Norman creation, nor does it mean that it was embroidered on the Norman side of the English Channel. It does suggest that the Tapestry expresses a will for peace that may have been shared by both Anglo-Saxons and Normans who may also have worked together in assembling the necessary mate-

Stone frieze with sword and armor from Old Minster, Winchester

© JOHN CROOK AND WINCHESTER EXCAVATIONS COMMITTEE

rials and blending them into an embroidery. Leaving aside for the moment the fact that England and Normandy were a single entity after the Conquest, it is hard to imagine an undertaking of the magnitude of the Tapestry without the consent and active support of the Normans. After all, it took the thirty-five women of the Leek Embroidery Society thirteen months to sew a reproduction, and this time was shortened because the design was taken from the original (see p. 83). It is equally difficult to imagine the actual embroidery upon linen without the skill traditionally ascribed to Anglo-Saxon textile workers. So we are left with a view of the Bayeux Tapestry that resists the will to make it either English or French. We are left with a Tapestry that is mixed and international and with a work of art with a longer reach than what was available in the proximate cultural environment of either England or France. For one of the ways that a peaceful blending of peoples might come about is through the focus upon a common enemy or a third term, which for the makers of the Tapestry, as well as for Normans after the Conquest, was to be found in the Middle East. It is to the Tapestry's Eastern elements and to the world of Byzantine silks that we now turn.

CHAPTER 6

WEAVING
TO
BYZANTIUM

AMONG THE CONTENDERS FOR THE ENGLISH CROWN UPON
Edward the Confessor's death in 1066, Harold Godwineson and
Duke William of Normandy were not alone. The Scandinavians
who had ruled Britain off and on for almost two centuries before
Edward's reign, the centuries sometimes called the Viking Age,
laid claim to England alongside the Anglo-Saxons and Normans.
King Harald Hardråda of Norway, in league with Harold Godwineson's older brother Tostig, swept down from the North as
William was preparing to cross the English Channel. William
carried the day at Hastings because of superb diplomatic and military preparation, because of superior tactics and daring, because
of the lucky arrow that landed in Harold's eye. But William was
one of those conquering figures—like Alexander the Great, Caesar, or Charlemagne—whom history favors, at least for a while,
and as luck would have it, King Harald Hardråda's attack upon
King Harold at Stamford Bridge, near the town of York, so weak-
ened the English that it was an important factor in William's victory at Hastings just two weeks later. Harald Hardråda was a
formidable foe, and had things turned out differently at the Battle of Stamford Bridge, William, whose ancestors were Scandinavian, would have faced a fellow Norseman at Hastings. The story
of Harald Hardråda's early adventures in the Mediterranean has
special meaning for our understanding of Hastings and of the
Bayeux Tapestry's debt not only to Anglo-Saxon, Norman, and
Scandinavian culture, but to that of the Middle East.

On July 29, 1030, Harald Hardråda, only fifteen years old, fought alongside his half-brother King Olaf of Norway at the Battle of Stiklestad. Olaf, who had been baptized in Rouen, Normandy, France, and had traveled as a Viking to England, met his death, though he would later be resurrected as Saint Olaf. Harald was only wounded and escaped into the Norwegian woods. Hidden by farmers, he "crept from forest to forest" until he reached Sweden, and from Sweden he sailed to Russia, where he and his retainers were received at Novgorod by King Jaroslav. The Norwegians stayed for several years at the Russian court before making their way in the mid-1030s to Greece and Constantinople, where, in the phrase of the thirteenth-century Icelandic poet Snorri Sturluson, "His swan-breasted ships swept / Towards the tall-towered city."[1] Harald "presented himself to the Empress of Byzantium and immediately joined her army." In short order, he was the captain of the Varangians, the emperor's personal guard composed of Scandinavian mercenaries.

The Norwegian and Russian courts were models of stability compared with the world in which Harald found himself, known even in the eleventh century for its "Byzantine" complications, for treachery and intrigue. One of the keenest observers of the imperial court at Constantinople, Michael Psellus, a tutor and adviser to successive emperors, summarizes his firsthand knowledge of the regime in the years covering Harald's time in the East: "Not one of the emperors in my time—and I say this with experience of many in my life, for most of them only lasted a year—not one of them, to my knowledge, bore the burden of Empire entirely free from blame to the end. Some were naturally evil, others were evil through their friendship for certain individuals, and others again for some other of the common reasons."[2]

So corrupt was the Byzantine court that, beginning in 988 when Emperor Basil II received a contingent of "Scythians" from the Taurus in Russia to help him suppress the rebellion of his former ally Bardas Phocas, the emperor surrounded himself with outsiders, "ax bearers" from the North. The name "Varangian" derives from the Old Norse *vár,* "pledge," and was first applied to Scandinavians who came to fight for the rulers of Kiev and Novgorod. As "Men of the Pledge," the Varangians were known for keeping their word. Anna Comnena, daughter of Emperor Alexius I, observes in the biography of her famous father (the *Alexiad*) that "the Varangians, who bear on their shoulders the heavy iron sword, regard loyalty to the emperors and the protection of their persons as a family tradition, a kind of sacred trust and inheritance handed down from generation to generation."[3]

In the ten years Harald served as a Varangian in the Mediterranean, he fought in Africa among the Saracens, where he captured, according to the Icelandic saga that bears his name, eighty cities. From Africa Harald moved to Sicily, where he "garnered an immense hoard of money, gold and treasure of all kinds." As Harald amassed booty, he sent it by "his own reliable messengers" back to Novgorod into the safekeeping of King Jaroslav. Harald returned to Constantinople but did not stay very long. He left for Jerusalem, where he conquered Palestine in what appears as a foretaste of the First Crusade. Harald bathed in the river Jordan before returning to Constantinople. In one of his poems, Harald mentions having visited a "town in the south," possibly Athens, which is at the source of the legend that Harald etched the runic letters on a great marble lion from Piraeus, now in Venice, though the letters themselves do not bear this out.

Again in Constantinople around 1046, Harald announced his plans to return north, and the empress had him imprisoned. Writing in the thirteenth century, the saga poet Snorri Sturluson, in a psychohistorical interpretation of events that had occurred two centuries earlier, surmises that the empress was secretly in love with him. Harald eventually did escape, however, through his courage and cleverness—and through a miracle. While in prison, he had a vision of his dead half-brother Olaf. That very night, the Scandinavian prisoners were visited by the servants of a woman who had once been healed by Olaf, who had also appeared to her in a dream and "directed her to rescue his brother Harald."

The liberated Varangians avenged themselves by putting out the emperor's eyes, then they carried off the empress's niece and sped to their galleys. All that remained by way of barrier was the great iron chain across the Bosporus. As his boats approached the chain, Harald ordered those of his men who were rowing to ply their oars as fast as they could, while the others were to move to the stern with all their goods. When the prow of the ship became stuck upon the iron links, he commanded those in the stern to rush to the prow, thus pivoting his "dragon" upon the fulcrum used to prevent enemies from reaching Constantinople. Harald's boat escaped unharmed, while the other ship "stuck fast on the chains and broke its back. Many of her crew were lost, but some were rescued from the sea."

From Constantinople, Harald made his way back to Novgorod, where he reclaimed the gold and "valuable treasure of all kinds" sent there from Greece, Africa, Sicily, and Palestine. "This hoard of wealth was so immense that no one in northern Europe had ever seen the like of it in one man's possession before." He left for Sweden, having married King Jaroslav's daughter, one of whose sisters married the king of Hungary and the other the king of France. When Harald, after plundering in Denmark, eventually returned to Norway, it was as co-regent with Olaf's son Magnus, from whom he had purchased half the realm with the booty amassed in the East: "Harald had a huge ox-hide spread out on the floor, and the gold was emptied onto it out of the chests. . . . All those present were astonished that such immense wealth in gold should have been assembled in Scandinavia in one place." At Magnus's death, Harald laid claim to Denmark in addition to Norway, and it was Harald who in the spring of 1066 joined forces with Harold Godwineson's brother Tostig, Earl of Northumbria, to lay claim, in the line of Danes who had ruled England off and on for over two centuries, to half of England as well.

Harald's itinerary—from Norway, to Russia, to Constantinople, Africa, and Sicily, then back to Norway and, finally, to Britain—shows the permeability of northern and southern worlds. And though Harald was exceptional, he was not alone. In the century of the Norman Conquest, northern merchants, clerics, pilgrims, warriors, and even some free farmers traveled by rivers and overland portage across what is now Russia or by sea through the Straits of Gibraltar to the Middle East, northern Italy, Rome, Jerusalem, and Constantinople, where they traded, prayed, and fought like Harald in the emperor's guard. In 957, Helga or Olga of Kiev visited Constantinople; in 990, the Icelander Thorvald the Far-Travelled, a missionary converted by the Saxons, made a pilgrimage to Jerusalem, returning via Syria and Byzantium. The thirteenth-century Icelandic *Njal's Saga* tracks the voyage of Kolskegg, whose itinerary is very much like that of Harald. "Kolskegg was baptized in Denmark. But he never found happiness there, and moved on east to Russia, where he stayed for one winter. From there he travelled to Constantinople where he joined the Emperor's army. The last that was heard of him was that he had married there and become a leader in the Varangian Guard. He stayed there for the rest of his life; and he is now out of this saga."[4]

Runic characters incised in stones of the Middle East and in stones erected especially in Sweden and Gotland commemorate beloved family members who died in faraway Constantinople, or "Micklegarth." The Norse name "Halfdan" is incised in a marble screen of the south gallery of Hagia Sophia. A stone in Fjuckby, Uppland, was placed there by Liutr the pilot in memory of his sons: "One was named Ake, who perished while abroad . . . he sailed into Greek ports. . . ." A stone in Ärlinghundra, Uppland, was erected by Härlev and Torgerd, whose father, Säbjörn, "commanded a boat in the East with Ingvar. . . ." On another, Tjälve and Hlomlög ordered stones for their son who "owned a boat and sailed it East. . . ." A runic inscription from Östergötland, Sweden, around A.D. 800 marks the death of Øyvind, who "fell in the East" with a companion.[5]

As we see in the Bayeux Tapestry, Harold II of England had himself crowned the day after Edward the Confessor's death, alleging in the scene visible in the upper part of panel 70, where Edward's relatives are gathered, that the dying Edward had left him the crown and kingdom upon his deathbed. Harold's older brother Tostig, who controlled the army at the time of what he considered to be Harold's usurpation, left immediately, according to the chronicler Orderic Vitalis, for Normandy, where he secured Duke William's permission to return to England. William, calculating and clever as he was, encouraged Tostig without offering anything more concrete, knowing that an attack upon Harold from whatever source would weaken him and would make William's ambitions in England easier to realize. "But it is written," Orderic reminds us, that " 'Man proposes, God disposes,' and things fell out otherwise than they planned."[6] Tostig found himself neither strong enough to enter England nor able to return to Normandy because of unfavorable weather.

"Tossed about by the west and south and other winds," Tostig proceeded to Flanders, Frisia, and Denmark, seeking help in taking back the kingdom that he saw as belonging as rightfully to him as to his brother Harold. Tostig might have gone to Flanders because his father, Godwine, had sought and received refuge there when forced to flee at the height of his own troubles with King Edward in 1051–1052 and because he was married to Judith, daughter of Count Baldwin of Flanders. Yet Flanders was also an unlikely source for aid in conquering England, since William of Normandy was married to Baldwin's daughter Mathilda. From Flanders, Tostig went to Denmark, where he reminded the Danish king Sweyn that his uncle Cnut had ruled England and that, were the two to unite, half of England might be his. In an uncharacteristic show of modesty and restraint within the world of Icelandic sagas, Sweyn replied that "as far as I am concerned, I intend to be guided more by my own limitations than by my uncle Cnut's achievements."

Tostig left for Norway, where, as the chronicler Orderic Vitalis tells us, he pleaded with King Harald Hardråda: " 'Great king, I approach your throne as a suppliant, offering myself and my service in good faith to your majesty, in the hope of being restored by your aid to the honour which is mine by right of inheritance. For Harold my brother, who ought rightly to obey me as the firstborn, has treacherously risen against me and presumptuously on false pretences made himself king of England. Therefore I seek help from you as your liegeman, knowing that you have a strong army and every military virtue. Destroy my brother's upstart strength in war, keep half England for yourself, and let me have the other half to hold as your faithful vassal as long as I live.' "[7] Tostig's proposal fell on receptive ears. "The earl and the king talked together often and at length; and finally they came to the decision to invade England that summer."[8]

This was, of course, the summer of William's shipbuilding and amassing of a fleet on the river Dives, as seen in Tapestry panels 83–86. From Dives, William moved his armada, estimated at between seven hundred and one thousand ships (though the chronicler William of Jumièges reckoned it at three thousand), to the ancient Roman port of Saint-Valery at the mouth of the river Somme, in order to take advantage of a shorter crossing. There, according to his chaplain and biographer, William of Poitiers,

Duke William sat for several weeks, prevented by unfavorable winds from setting sail. He prayed, he sighed, he made pious offerings, he had "the body of Valery, a confessor most acceptable to God, carried out of the basilica to quell the contrary wind and bring a favourable one."[9] But, above all, William watched the church's weathercock, a gesture that may be alluded to in the Tapestry on panel 66, where a workman, in placing the finishing touch upon a large building project, sets a weathercock atop Westminster Abbey. "You looked to see by what wind the weathercock of the church was turned," the author of *The Song of the Battle of Hastings* addresses William. "If the south wind blew, at once you returned thence joyful; if suddenly the north wind diverted and held off the south, lamenting, you bedewed your face with welling tears."[10]

The same wind that prevented William from crossing the English Channel blew Harald Hardråda's forces down from the North. The Norwegian king arrived off the river Tyne with some three hundred ships. Joined by Tostig, who had spent the summer raiding like a Viking along the northern coast, Harald Hardråda entered the mouth of the river Humber sometime around September 18. At Gate Fulford outside the city of York, the combined Norwegian and rebellious English forces met Earls Edwin and Morcar and defeated the Mercian army in what was the first of three great battles of the year 1066. King Harold of England, meanwhile, had learned of the invasion in the North and marched with full force toward York. There negotiations took place, in the course of which Harold is said to have offered Harald Hardråda "six feet of English soil, or seven, since he is reported to be bigger than most men."

On September 25, 1066, at Stamford Bridge, the English army defeated and killed both Harald Hardråda and Harold's brother Tostig in as complete a victory as any of the Middle Ages.

Harald Hardråda, known as "the Thunderbolt of the North," was the last of the great Viking leaders. He used his military might to amass wealth with which he eventually purchased kingship. His travels, in fact, can be traced by the Byzantine coins he left in his wake. A coin that Harald received from Emperor Michael IV as a reward for his participation in the campaign against the Bulgarians may have been the model for the Danish silver penny of Sweyn Estridsen, struck around 1047, as well as for many copies of Byzantine coins produced in Denmark.[11] In an addition to the eleventh-century *History of the Archbishops of Hamburg,* Adam of Bremen makes the claim that Harald Hardråda took his great treasure with him to England on his final expedition. So if we follow the money, the wealth that weighed so much, in Adam's words, that "twelve young men could hardly lift it to their shoulders" fell into the hands of Harold Godwineson.[12]

King Harold Godwineson's victory at Stamford Bridge was bittersweet, however. Within a matter of days, he learned that on the morning of September 28, Duke William of Normandy had landed in the old Roman port of Pevensey, not knowing, of course, whether he would face Harald of Norway or Harold of England. From his encampment, William began pillaging the countryside, as depicted in Tapestry panels 104–108. That William plundered in the part of England that was the ancestral seat of the Godwine family and belonged to Harold both as king and as Earl of Kent must have added to the ignominy of the news.

How did word reach Harold in the North?

The Song of the Battle of Hastings tells of a peasant hiding under a rock by the sea, where he observed the Norman landing. Upon mounting his horse, he rode toward York and encountered Harold "returning from battle, laden with rich spoils. The messenger rushed to meet him and poured out the tale he bore in this way. 'O King, truly I bring you fearful news! The duke of the Normans, with Frenchmen and Bretons, has invaded the land; he is ravaging and burning. If you ask how many thousands he has, no one will be able to tell you. . . . He is seizing boys and girls, and the widows also; and at the same time all the beasts.' "[13] In panel 106 of the Tapestry, we see what appears to be the slaughter of livestock, and in 118 the Normans torch a house from which a woman and child flee. The Tapestry images of William's plunder in Kent could not be further from the reputation his army had earned in the weeks of waiting in Saint-Valery, where, in the words of William of Poitiers, "the cattle and flocks of the people of the province grazed safely, . . . and the crops waited unharmed for the scythe of the harvester."

Harold's moves after the Battle of Stamford Bridge are difficult to know with certainty. If he decided to move south only after hearing the news of William's landing, which could not have reached York before October 1, his army covered the 180 miles to London in just five days. After spending five or six days in London in an effort to recruit reinforcements, the English army must have left London on October 11 in order to cover the fifty-eight miles from London to Hastings, where they arrived, exhausted, on October 13, 1066.

Harald Hardråda and Tostig's challenge near York and the extraordinary march to Hastings were determining factors in Harold of England's loss of life and crown the very next day. He had made a series of tactical mistakes. He did not wait until he could replenish his troops and overwhelm the Norman invaders with numbers. He did not prepare for a defensive war, since he conceived of himself as the attacker. Harold brought to Hastings approximately seven thousand troops against William's slightly fewer knights, archers, foot soldiers, and auxiliaries. The small difference in numbers was inflected, however, by an imbalance in the competence and quality as well as the preparedness of the opposing troops. Harold had left his best and most seasoned men in the North; and William had a much higher percentage of professional warriors and a larger contingent of archers.

The Tapestry treats in some detail the events preceding the Battle of Hastings—scouting, negotiation, and positioning. In panel 117, William is informed of Harold's arrival. In panels 122–128, the Norman troops ride to encounter those of Harold. The inscription over panel 127 reads, "William questions Vital if he has seen Harold's army." A helmetless Norman figure on top of a hill in panel 130 performs reconnaissance, while an English figure, hand raised to his eyes in a gesture meant to enhance vision, spots the Normans in panel 132. Harold is informed of the presence of William's army in panel 133.

Chronicle accounts insist upon William's offer, delivered by a Norman monk, "to accept a judgement determined by the laws of peoples" (William of Poitiers), to submit to "the decision of the Holy See, or to ordeal by battle" (William of Malmesbury). In the words of his biographer William of Poitiers, William "did not wish the English to die as enemies on account of his dispute; he wished to decide the case by risking his own head in single combat." "But," writes William of Malmesbury, twelfth-century chronicler of English kings, "there was no holding Harold. Rash as he was, he refused to lend a patient ear to good advice, thinking it discreditable and a blot upon his record to turn tail in the face of any danger. With the same impudence, or—to put it more kindly—imprudence, he sent packing the monk who had come as an emissary from William, refusing in his passion even to receive him with civility; he merely expressed the wish that God might judge between himself and William."

At about the third hour, or 9:00 A.M., on October 14, William's Norman knights met the ax-wielding Anglo-Saxon foot soldiers of King Harold's army. Tapestry panel 134 shows William giving the order of attack, which is received in stages as the command is transmitted. As in a slow-motion film in which the events of a

single moment are suspended, words are transformed into action—the first clash of battle, shown in panel 144.

The Tapestry's depiction of battle is generally accurate, to
judge by the chronicle accounts that speak of Hastings at a temporal remove of between ten years for William of Poitiers's *Gesta
Guillelmi,* to twenty years for Amatus of Montecassino's *History of
the Normans,* to over a century for Robert Wace's *Roman de Rou.* At
first, William failed to break Harold's defense, Harold having the
advantage of the high ground on Senlac Hill, as seen in panel 157.
William's army was supposedly demoralized, and the rumor circulated that its leader had been killed. Bishop Odo is seen rallying the troops in panel 158, and William shows himself in panel
160. Harold, who, tacticians say, should have advanced and attacked, was unable to control his army, which sensed that victory
had been achieved, and he abandoned the main body of the army
on the hill to pursue William's troops. In the chaos of battle, bril-
liantly portrayed in the upended horses and tumbling riders of
panels 155 and 156, and in the back-and-forth of action in panels
156–167, William's army, aided by the mobility of mounted
knights, managed to turn and feign flight in order to entice the
defenders from the hill. Then, turning once more, William
charged up the hill and, in the phrase of William of Poitiers, "cut
them to pieces."

It was then that Harold, alongside his brothers Gyrth and
Leofwine, was killed, struck through the eye by an arrow launched
by one of the eighteen archers shown in the border beneath panels 160–164. The account of the arrow through Harold's eye is
not a contemporary one and first appears in Amatus of Montecassino's *History of the Normans.* Other accounts claim Harold died
early in the day and was hacked to death. *The Song of the Battle of
Hastings* contains the most vivid description, according to which
William "pierced the king's chest with his lance," Eustache of
Bologne cut off his head, Hugh of Ponthieu "liquified his entrail

with a spear," and Giffard "cut off his thigh and carried it some distance away." The dismemberment lends some credence to the chronicles that claim Harold's body to have been so disfigured that his wife, Edith, had to be called to identify it "by certain marks." The Norman victory was complete, as the ragged English in the Tapestry's final segment flee into the tatters of its damaged final edge. Harald Hardråda's coin horde, amassed in the Middle East and gathered by Harold of England after the Battle of Stamford Bridge, fell into the hands of King William, whose mints after the Conquest struck coins of the Byzantine type.

Panel 144 is remarkable for what it reveals about the event of 1066, and it contains an extraordinary moment of visual turning in the Tapestry itself. At the very instant that the first Norman lance touches the first Anglo-Saxon body and in the space between lance and shield, the varied and exotic decoration of the lower border—fables, ornamental spirals, chevrons, palmettes, acanthus leaves, and exotic animals—yields to dead bodies and body parts, arms and armor, fallen horses, the detritus of war. The pair of birds facing each other in panel 143 just before physical contact lose their balance, are tipped backward, upended. It is as if the Tapestry Master sought to mark the moment at which civil and political dealings conducted in words—royal and ducal councils, messages, last wishes, oaths, orders, and negotiations—gave way to the physicality of bodies and battle.

The border that to this point had been ruled off from the main panels as a separate decorative space suddenly opens, dropping like a trap, to join the plane of action as the ground and foreground of the carnage at Hastings. Fighters move on this plane amid the slaughter. In panel 158, a knight defends himself with his shield. The Norman archers of panels 160–164 stand upon this ground. Figures in panels 167, 168, and 171 strip fallen bodies of their coats of mail. Nor is this the first opening of the ground beneath the main panels. The border disappears beneath panel 45 as William and Harold cross the treacherous river Couesnon, and men slip into sand riddled with eels and snakes. To the right in lower 46, a lion attacks the leg of a fallen knight. The disappearance of the ruling that separates the main panels from the lower border signifies a loss of footing in the world, an inability to stand on firm ground, a mingling of men and mud, of men, reptiles, and beasts.

What follows in the border beneath panel 144 is all business, horror, inhumanity, an unspeakable scene of death and dismemberment, in which Norman and Anglo-Saxon bodies are mixed and human bodies are mixed with dead animals. What lies in the lower border before panel 144 is just the opposite—decoration implying leisure, fables, or the stuff of literature, a tempering of events, a slowing of the eye distracted from the forward march of history in the main panels, cultural play.

The figures in both the upper and the lower margins, separated by the ornament of diagonal bars, spirals, and decorative floral elements, consist for the most part of pairs of accosted animals—that is, animals facing each other in what appears sometimes to be a posture of attack and at other times a more gentle pairing—as well as addorsed animals, aligned back-to-back: lions with their tails raised and lions with their tails in their mouths; tigers with tails raised in upper 8; winged dragons in lower 31; wyverns—a winged dragon with feet like those of an eagle and a serpentlike barbed tail—in lower 135 and lower 48; griffins—a fabulous animal with the head and wings of an eagle and the body and hindquarters of a lion—in lower 85 and 92 as well as upper 15 and 106; griffins with tails raised in upper 24; winged horses above panels 134–135; birds of various species—vultures in panel 107 under the scene of Norman plunder, storks with their heads in the ground under panel 91, cranes under panel 56; centaurs—

creatures with a human head and the body of a horse—in upper 25; winged centaurs below panel 3; roosters in upper 26; rams in upper 27; deer in upper 29; camels in upper 32; peacocks in upper 37; boars in upper 46.

The animals in the margins of the Tapestry are impressive in their number—87 pairs in the lower border from the beginning until the first shock of battle, 120 pairs in the upper border from beginning until the end, for a total of 207 pairs, or 414 animals in all, not counting, of course, the animals in the fables and the hunting and hunted animals in the margins. And the animals are astonishing in their variety. Some are real and domestic—roosters, rams, deer, and boars. Some are real and exotic—lions, camels, and peacocks. A good number are creatures of the imagination from medieval bestiaries, animal books inherited from the ancient world—dragons, centaurs, griffins, and wyverns.

The beasts in the borders are most striking, however, in their symmetry. Though they appear in a variety of positions and with a variety of attributes relative to other pairs, the animals of any given pair—accosted, addorsed, accosted and looking back or away from each other, addorsed and looking back toward each other—are consistently symmetrical. The striped tigers of upper panel 8 both show a lowered head and raised tail in a twisted posture meant to mimic each other. The facing lions in upper 16 both assume the rampant position, head and tail raised, front paws in the air. Of the facing wyverns in upper 41, each has hoisted its tail over its shoulder. The upended birds in upper 117 are reflections of each other. When the wings of a bird assume an unnatural position, that position is regularly reproduced by its paired mate, as in the outstretched wings on the birds in upper 5 and 138 or the single extended wing in upper 130–131. The facing cranes in lower 56 both have their beaks in the air; the facing cranes of upper 128 both have their beaks in the sand.

In several instances, an animal pair seems to escape the borders and move to the center of the Tapestry, as in the accosted birds with head feathers raised under the motte-and-bailey castle of Dol in panel 47, the accosted sheep or dogs under the motte-and-bailey at Rennes in panel 49, or, under the motte-and-bailey of Dinan in 52, the accosted knights whose swords, shields, banners, and torches are aligned so symmetrically that they seem to be moving in some kind of destructive dance. The pair of birds atop the cornice of the balustrade where Harold sits to hear the news of the appearance of a comet in panel 75 are integrated to the Tapestry as architectural ornament. Elsewhere, the pairing is erotic and even parodic, as in the accosted naked man and woman in the lower border of panel 30 and in the upper border of panels 123–124—couples of lovebirds whose presence renders visible the ambiguity of the animal twosomes of the Tapestry. Accosted in one way, the animals in the margins are prepared to fight; accosted in another, they are, arms outstretched like birds with raised symmetrical wings, ready to make love.

The symmetry of the animals in the upper and lower borders, their luxurious ornamental status, and the exoticism of tigers, winged lions, lions with tails raised, centaurs, griffins, dragons, wyverns, camels, and peacocks reorient our understanding of the Bayeux Tapestry in the direction of the Mediterranean and the Middle East. More precisely, they guide us toward the one source by which such images might have been known in the eleventh century, or before they will become such an integral part of the system of heraldic signs in the twelfth—the world of Byzantine silks. The great shaping reservoir of ornamental, symmetrical, exotic animal imagery are the woven silks that circulated throughout Western Europe in the centuries before the Norman Conquest. The Bayeux Tapestry owes much more to Byzantium than to the Scandinavian textiles found at Oseberg and Rolvsøy,

Norway, or the linen from Överhogdal, Sweden, which them-selves were inflected by the prestige of weavings from the East.

The Tapestry and silks were designed for display on the walls of public or domestic space. Though we do not know whether the Tapestry was intended to hang in a church or palace, it is difficult to imagine any means of display other than that of a wall hanging. Similarly, we can tell by the length of the pattern repeats in many silks from the eighth through the eleventh centuries that they were woven to be hung in the large spaces of a church, on walls, in front of doors or the presbytery, in the nave arcades, or around the arched vault over the high altar.

Emperor Justinian (ruled 527–565) gave to the Church of Saint Sophia in Constantinople a large quantity of precious cloth woven with gold, precious stones, and pearls. Some of the cloths were meant to cover liturgical objects such as the chalice and the Eucharist dish, or paten. Others were suspended between the columns of the recessed area reserved for the Eucharist. Sant'Apollinare Nuovo in Ravenna, a sixth-century church mod-eled on the buildings of the East, contains a mosaic showing decorative hangings over the doors and between the columns of the Great Palace of Constantinople (see insert, figure 4). The churches of Rome were filled with silks. In the early ninth cen-tury, Pope Leo III (papacy, 795–816) draped a "rather large gold embroidered, purple veil, which hangs from the silver beam be-fore the image of the Saviour, over the entry to the vestibule" of Saint Peter's. Figural hangings are noted under Pope Gregory IV (papacy, 827–844), "Alexandrian veils hanging in front of the main door with men and horses." Pope Sergius II (844–847) had "three purple silk covers" placed over icons. Pope Stephen VI (papacy, 885–891) presented to Saint Peter's "ninety silk hang-ings with lion motifs, [one hanging] for each presbytery arch."[14]

The Tapestry and Byzantine silks are similar in that both are examples of mixed media. Of the hundreds of pieces of silk that survive from what must surely have been thousands, many contain inscriptions. Writing on silk, or writing woven into silk, is an Eastern phenomenon and distinguishes the world of Byzantine silks from that of Scandinavian textiles, which show no trace of written inscription. However, the inscriptions on surviving fragments of Greek silk, unlike those of the Tapestry, give some indication of their origin. All five of the imperial lion silks to have reached the West between the middle of the ninth century and the first quarter of the eleventh reveal in Greek letters the reign under which they were made. On the Siegburg lion silk is written, "During the reign of Romanos and Christophoros, the Christ loving rulers"; on the Crefeld-Berlin-Düsseldorf and Cologne lion silks, "During the reign of Constantine and Basile, the Christ loving rulers"; on the Auxerre lion silk, "During the reign of Leo, the Christ-loving ruler." The Aachen elephant silk contains two inscriptions, one partially unreadable: "In the time of Michael, . . ." and "When Peter was the archon of Zeuxippos, indiction . . ." The inscriptions on Byzantine silks are on the order of a signature, and though one cannot tell who actually made them, one knows under whose command they were made, silk production being an imperial monopoly.

The Tapestry inscriptions seem to yield relatively more information about who appears where on its surface, and in places they even hint at the nature of the actions depicted. Yet they are in their way also remarkably mute. They yield little essential information about the key dramatic moments and issues around which the events leading to the Battle of Hastings actually turn. They give no indication of the Tapestry's origin. Rather, they serve as place markers, orienting us geographically or temporally within the long embroidered scroll. Beginning often with the Latin UBI ("Where") or HIC ("Here"), they point to where a par-

ticular action or exchange takes place: UBI UNUS CLERICUS ET
ÆLFGYVA ("Where a cleric and Ælfgyva"); UBI HAROLD SACRA-
MENTUM FECIT WILLELMO DUCI ("Where Harold swore an
oath to Duke William"); HIC HAROLD DUX REVERSUS EST AD
ANGLICAM TERRAM ET VENIT AD EDWARDUM REGEM ("Here
Duke Harold returned to England and came to King Edward");
HIC EDWARDUS REX IN LECTO ALLOQUITUR FIDELES ("Here
King Edward in bed speaks with his faithful"); and HIC
DEDERUNT HAROLDO CORONAM REGIS ("Here they have given
the crown of king to Harold").

The inscriptions of the Bayeux Tapestry are enticing, but they
promise more information than they actually deliver. Though we
learn the name of the mysterious lady Ælfgyva in panel 39, we still
wonder about the cleric with her and why he touches Ælfgyva's
head. An inscription tells us that Harold swore an oath to
William, but nothing about what was sworn. We learn via writing
that Harold came to William upon his return to England, but
nothing about the nature of their council. The Tapestry's script
tells us that Edward spoke to his faithful on his deathbed but remains quiet about the nature of any deathbed confession or testament, words at the core of the dispute over royal succession and
William's invasion of England. An inscription reveals that "they
have given the crown" to Harold, without revealing who exactly
has made him king or under what jurisdiction.

The discretion of the Tapestry's inscriptions supports the
claim that the deepest intention and effect of this multifaceted
work of art is to allow the widest possible range of interpretation
and thus the widest field of identification among viewers with
the widest set of investments and interests. Norman, Anglo-
Saxon, or Scandinavian—each can read anything desired into the
empty vessels of inscription. And whatever is projected upon it
by way of meaning will be united with other such projections that
meet on the surface of the embroidery. The Tapestry's openness

binds those who see it and read its inscriptions into a single people by offering something for all while excluding and subduing
none. Each can walk away thinking that his party is represented,
which is also why scholars through the ages have been able to
maintain with apparent rigor equal and opposite points of view
regarding the Tapestry's commission, purpose, and date and place
of creation.

Some of the scenes and images from the Tapestry derive from the
Byzantine world, if not directly from silks. While the portrayal of
Harold in majesty, discussed in relation to Continental elements
of the Tapestry's design, was characteristic of the way the Germanic emperors represented themselves, the Ottonian and
Salian kings learned about frontality from the Greeks. The orans
position of Archbishop Stigand next to Harold is found in the
crypt of San Clemente at Rome, yet before that, it was set into
the byzantinizing apse mosaic of Saint Apollinaris as orant in
sixth-century Ravenna. The scene of King Edward on his
deathbed in panel 70 resembles the set scene of the Dormition of
the Virgin on her bier, surrounded by mourning apostles on
Byzantine embroideries from the tenth century on. The Dormition is to the East what the Virgin's Assumption is to the West.

   The curious masthead of William's ship, the *Mora,* in its crossing of the English Channel in panel 98, consisting as it does of a
small cross atop a square frame with another cross within its
equilateral sides, is very much like the cross carried by a crowned
emperor, a rigid standard atop a pole, on the silk belonging to the
diocese museum of Bamberg Cathedral (see insert, figure 5). As
in the main panels of the Tapestry, the moving figures of the
Bamberg silk are framed by borders with medallions enclosing
foliate and geometric designs; and like the Tapestry, it shows the
capacity of Byzantine weavers to carry out large figurative com-

positions, possibly even of a contemporary event, and not just or-namental repeats. This silk, from the grave of Bishop Gunther, is datable between the year 1017 and Gunther's death in 1065. Gunther died in Hungary while returning from a diplomatic mis-sion to Constantinople on behalf of Henry IV, and it is possible that the Bamberg silk was a gift from the Byzantine emperor Constantine X (ruled 1059–1067) to his German counterpart. Had Bishop Gunther not died on his way home and had he not died in 1065, envoys sent by William to secure Henry IV's sup-port for the invasion of England might have seen this silk when they visited the imperial court in 1066.

What the Bayeux Tapestry takes most consistently from im-perial Byzantine silks are the accosted and addorsed animals along its upper and lower borders. A silk from the shrine of Saint Anno, who died in 1075, was translated to Siegburg, Germany, along with the saint's relics in 1183, though the inscription places its weaving between 921 and 931. The Siegburg silk shows con-fronted lions with raised tails. A lion silk that was removed from a shrine holding the relics of Saint Heribert, archbishop of Cologne, who died in 1021, shows a very similar couple (see in-sert, figure 6).

Imperial lion silks are joined by pieces containing confronted elephants. An imperial silk from the Aachen, Munster, treasury taken from the shrine of Charlemagne in 1843, though not origi-nally buried with him, shows decorated elephants wearing a sad-dle with a bilateral tree behind them. Each elephant is contained within a floriated roundel, with smaller circular floral designs in the space between circles. An elephant silk currently in the Louvre, Paris, displays accosted elephants framed not by individ-ual medallions, but by a border like that of the Bayeux Tapestry, containing geometric patterns and interlace, an ornamental string of hearts, a Kufic—decorative Arabic writing—inscription, and a train of camels at its leftmost edge (see insert, figure 7).

Under the feet of each elephant is a winged animal with four legs, the head of a dragon, and a raised tail. We know from the inscription, which reads, "Glory and prosperity to the Qa'id Abu Mansur Bukhtakin, may God prolong his existence," that the Paris elephant silk was executed no later than the mid–tenth century, since Abu Mansur was put to death in 961.

Griffins also figure in the menagerie of symmetrical animals. An addorsed rearing pair with heads looking back at each other belongs to the cathedral treasury of Sion, Switzerland (see insert, figure 8). The use of murex, or "true purple," dye in this weaving, once the lower edge of a dalmatic, speaks for a tenth- or eleventh-century imperial manufacture. A pair so upended that not even their rear feet seem to be on the ground belongs to Le Monastier, Haute-Loire, France. Thought to have been woven in tenth-century Constantinople, this piece of the shroud of Saint Chaffre shows quadrupeds suspended from the beak of each griffin and between them a tree on whose branches sit symmetrically posed birds and dogs. Between the wing and tail of each griffin are a pair of birds with griffinlike wings. Each repeat of this pattern contains no fewer than five mirrored pairs, ten animals in all.

Though the Saint Chaffre griffin is more complicated than silks with singly paired figures against an unfilled background, the weaving of even the simplest pattern is extremely complex. The design for the Aachen elephant silk, for example, required 1,440 manipulations of the heddle, the loom's pattern-producing device. This suggests that the symmetry of the exotic accosted and addorsed animals of the East is a function not of tradition or aesthetics, but of the technical manipulation of the pattern loom. In weaving the design in one direction, the weaver kept a record and simply reversed it in the figure harness mechanism to produce an image exactly the reverse of the original. The result is two images that reflect each other across the entire length of cloth.

A hunter silk from the same period, currently in the Museo Sacro, Vatican, features two pairs of hunters and their prey, separated by a tree, hunting dogs, birds, and trees filling the space within the spandrel, which itself contains geometric and foliate designs. The symmetry is obvious not only in the hunters' positions relative to their prey, which reflect each other along a horizontal axis (though the bottom pair is the opposite of the top), but in the equal extension of the tree over both, its trunk the central axis through which the pattern is mirrored from left to right. This must have been an astonishingly difficult design to execute, but it had to be designed only once. More precisely, only one-half of the whole had to be entered into the loom. The other half is a repetition in reverse of the first, and the repetition of the whole design is a repetition of this reversal.

The repetition of small figural or ornamental designs in woven textiles, whether integrally or in reverse, is so universal, even after the advent of the jacquard loom and mechanical means of executing a pattern, that it is impossible to say where and when it first began. Probably not in Byzantium or the Middle East but in China, whence silk arrived in Constantinople sometime around the middle of the sixth century and the repeat pattern loom a little later. The holding of a pattern in memory so that it might be repeated suggests an early relation between weaving and writing or the keeping of a written record of a particular design before the means were found to implement a pattern stored in the loom. It suggests, too, a relation between weaving and the enormous prestige attached to symmetrical designs in both the East and the West and in a wide range of media—carpets, manuscript illumination, wall painting, mosaics, architecture, and sculpture.

What was a technical reason for the accosted and addorsed animals of woven Byzantine silks, the repetition in reverse of a design on the repeat pattern loom, is not technical in the embroidered animals of the Bayeux Tapestry. An embroidered design, no matter how small, is drawn and stitched anew each time, and though the facing members of a pair may be symmetrical, they are never exactly the same as among the pixels of woven silk. Unlike in the main panels, where the shape of the Conquest story dictates the sequence of figural presentation, in the borders there is simply no practical reason why the animals face each other—except for one: that of prestige. What is a technical matter in the making of woven silks is for the embroidery of the Tapestry a matter of style. Byzantine silks, many of which served as borders for larger textiles, were luxury items par excellence associated throughout the centuries in question with the opulence of the East, with the might and mystery of the emperors of Byzantium, for whom silk making was an imperial privilege. Their designs were received into the Tapestry because of the status bestowed upon those who wore, owned, were buried in, or simply viewed the noble bestiary from the East.

The emperors of Constantinople held a monopoly over the goods that went into making silks, over their manufacture and purpose, including trade. Unauthorized use of the murex dye—"true purple"—that went into certain imperial pieces was punishable by death. The control of silk was considered a matter of state policy comparable to the keeping of military secrets. Emperor Constantine Porphyrogenitus warned his son against giving barbarians imperial cloth, imperial crowns, and the technique of Greek fire; this despite the fact that the Byzantines, according to legend, had stolen the first silkworms, smuggled out of China in the bamboo walking sticks of monks, in the reign of Justinian.

The emperors used silks as a form of currency, as a tool for the negotiation of foreign policy, and as gifts to ratify treaties and agreements. The release of precious silks, as the historian Robert Lopez succinctly phrases it, "extended to the grantee some of the power and prestige" that belonged to the emperor and to his people.[15] The silks that left Byzantium for the West as diplomatic gifts, part of a marriage arrangement, or by trade were used as court dress, ecclesiastical vestment, church hangings, shrouds for relics, decorations for books, seal bags, and burial palls.

Silks from Byzantium ended up in western France. Duke Richard I of Normandy (934–996) endowed the church at Fécamp with "Phrygian textiles" heavy with gold and emeralds, fine white linens, purple cloths mixed with gold, and silks decorated with embroidery. Many French and English words for textiles still betray the Eastern origins of actual cloth. The French word for silk, *samit,* derives from the Greek *hexamitos,* meaning "six-threaded," and yielded the English "samite." "Mousseline," a combination of silk with gold thread mentioned by Marco Polo, is from Mosul, Iraq. "Baldachin," a rich brocade, comes from the Italian for the city of Baghdad; *damasquin* and "damask," silk woven with elaborate designs and figures, come from Damascus, Syria.

Silks also reached Scandinavia. King Cnut II, who died in 1086, was buried at Odense in a purple silk that was no doubt of Byzantine manufacture, as were the silks in the grave of Bishop Absalon, buried at Sorø, Denmark, in 1201. In the Icelandic *Laxdaela Saga,* Bolli Bollison, a member of the emperor's guard, returned from Constantinople to Iceland with eleven companions. "They were all wearing scarlet and rode in gilded saddles; they were all fine looking men, but Bolli surpassed them all. He was wearing clothes of gold-embroidered silk which the Byzantine Emperor had given him, and over them a scarlet cloak. He was girt with the sword 'Leg-Biter,' its pommel now gold-embossed and the hilt bound with gold."[16]

Many Byzantine silks could be found in England of the tenth and eleventh centuries. The relics of Saint Cuthbert (635–687), translated to Chester-le-Street in 883 to protect them from Danish invasion, were "recognized" in the middle of the tenth century when King Æthelstan (ruled 924–939) and his brother Edmund added "two robes of Grecian workmanship." Abbot Ælfric of Eynsham claims that Anglo-Saxon merchants went abroad to purchase embroideries, silk, and other Eastern goods "useful to the King, to ealdormen, to the rich, and to the whole people." Plain tabby weaves have been excavated from tenth-century graves near Coppergate, York, and from Saltergate, Lincoln. A tabby silk weave with a bird design, taken from the tomb of Edward the Confessor at Westminster Abbey, could be the very piece of silk represented in the Bayeux Tapestry as the cloth in which Edward is wrapped on his deathbed or the shroud in which his body is carried for burial.

Some woven pieces reached Kent and, more precisely, Canterbury, where the Tapestry might have been made. Embroideries, probably of Byzantine origin, have been found in graves in Kent from the sixth and seventh centuries. The cathedral chapter house is repository to two dozen silks with various patterns—lions, griffins, eagles, peacocks, and other birds. Some remain intact, whole cloth, while others were at some point cut from larger pieces and used as bags for the seals attached to charters and other documents. Seal bags provide important information for the dating of a particular piece of silk because the date shown on the charter is a time before which the silk had to be made.

One of the Canterbury seal bags shows a double-headed eagle, the double-headed eagle also being a function of the repeat pattern loom, surrounded by a border of small birds in medallions, looking alternately left and right (see insert, figure 9). This silk was woven in Byzantium in the ninth or tenth century and was cut and transformed into a seal bag in the eleventh. Another Byzantine piece from Canterbury contains the design of an animal's head, a lion or tiger with a flat broad head and small ears. Whoever designed the Bayeux Tapestry might, in fact, have seen these two examples of Byzantine weaving. He certainly had the opportunity to encounter silks as altar cloths or decoration in a church, as ecclesiastical alb, dalmatic, chasuble, or stole, as book cover, or as seal bag either in Normandy or in England and, if in England, possibly even in Canterbury, Kent.

CHAPTER 7

GO EAST, YOUNG NORMAN

IT IS HARD TO IMAGINE THE EXTENT TO WHICH THE WORLD changed for Anglo-Saxons on October 14, 1066. Having sustained three bloody battles, Fulford, Stamford Bridge, and Hastings, the English nobility had been depleted by bloodshed, "its downfall," in the words of William the Conqueror's modern biographer David Douglas, "one of the best documented social transformations of the eleventh century."[1] Of all the land in England, after the Norman Conquest, only 8 percent remained the possession of those who held it in 1066, according to the survey William the Conqueror ordered in 1086, the Domesday Book. For Anglo-Saxons, the Conquest was doom: "So very thoroughly did he have the inquiry carried out," the Anglo-Saxon Laud Chronicle reads for the year 1085, "that there was not a single 'hide,' not one virgate of land, not even—it is shameful to record it, but it did not seem shameful to him to do—not even one ox, nor one cow, nor one pig which escaped notice in his survey."

Though the great majority of Anglo-Saxons submitted to Norman rule, many resisted. An anonymous thirteenth-century manuscript speaks of a group of nobles, inhabitants of that part of England known as the Danelaw because it had been ruled by Danes, who sent to the Danish king Sweyn to help them escape their conquerors. The leader of the embassy to Denmark was none other than "Godwinus iunior," King Harold's younger brother. A Scandinavian fleet arrived in 1069, and Sweyn himself in 1070, to harry the coast of Yorkshire and East Anglia, until William bribed the Danes to leave. Sweyn's death in the mid-1070s meant that help would not be forthcoming from the North. The Anglo-Saxons "groaned aloud," in the phrase of the historian Orderic Vitalis, "for their lost liberty, and plotted ceaselessly to find some way of shaking off a yoke that was so intolerable and unaccustomed."[2]

In one of the most astonishing examples of the fallout from Hastings, ten years after the Conquest, a large contingent of Anglo-Saxon landholders "turned into money all the estates that they had in England" and left their homeland in 350 boats.[3] They had no idea where they would land, but almost anywhere seemed preferable to servitude in what had been their home. The Icelandic *Saga of King Edward the Confessor* identifies the leader of the rebels as Sigurd, Earl of Gloucester, who with "a great force of many picked men" sailed along the coast of France, Spain, and through the Straits of Gibraltar into Norva-Sound—the Mediterranean. There they sacked cities in what is now Morocco, taking "so much fee in gold and silver that it was more even than what they had taken away with them from England." They captured the islands of Majorca and Minorca. From the Baleares, Sigurd's men stopped in Sicily and Sardinia, where they heard of great strife in Micklegarth—Constantinople. For the Anglo-Saxon freebooters, where there was strife, there was also opportunity for "great advancement."

Sigurd's men arrived in the harbor of Constantinople, which had been blocked by pagans "some winters after the fall of King Harold." Liberating the besieged city, they were welcomed by the emperor and inhabitants. "They stayed a while in Micklegarth, and set the realm of the Greek King free from strife." Some of the exiled Anglo-Saxons joined the emperor's personal guard, the very Varangians that the Norwegian Harald Hardråda had led and left some thirty years earlier. Others, having been independent chiefs while in England, found "that it was too small a career to grow old there in that fashion, that they had not a realm to rule over." They begged the Greek leader to "give them some towns or cities which they might own and their heirs after them." The emperor, not wishing "to strip other men of their estates," granted them land that had once belonged to him but that since had been captured by "heathen men free from tax and toll." Should they manage to retake the territory "some six days and nights' sail across the sea in the east and northeast from Micklegarth," the land "should be their own and their heirs after them."

After many battles, Sigurd's men were successful. The English exiles, landholders once again, established a new territory, which they named appropriately "Nova Anglia"—New England. The towns were to be called London and York "and by the names of other great towns in England." And so, in or around 1078, in the region identified by some historians as part of what is now the Crimea, we find the first New England, New London, and New York. As feisty as the New Englanders of the United States, the New Englanders of the Crimea were unwilling to live under Eastern religious rule, so they sent to Hungary for bishops and priests. Their fellow exiles who stayed in Constantinople as part of the emperor's Varangians were among the force that in 1082 fought back the attempt of Normans settled in Sicily to capture Byzantium, and in this way they participated in some small measure in resistance to further Norman conquest.

For the Anglo-Saxons who left England after the Battle of Hastings, it may have seemed that the world they knew had ended. For those who stayed, however, the world merely changed, and there is no better embodiment of such change than the Bayeux Tapestry, which both reflects a past historical moment and, by the very nature of that reflection, alters the universe into which it was received. The Tapestry records the events leading up to Hastings, but the way it figures them visually carries new ways of conceiving time, places new emphasis upon everyday life and the secular world, proffers a vision of history as a logically connected continuum, makes an unseen connection to the classical past, and sets the stage for Anglo-Norman ambitions in the Mediterranean and the Middle East. Understood as an instrument and not just an image of historical change, the Tapestry, like all truly founding works of art, operates deep in the zone where form is retained as perception, perception is embodied in ideas, and ideas generate actions and consequences within the wider world.

The first clash of the Battle of Hastings, shown in Bayeux Tapestry panel 144, is an extraordinary historical moment, capturing as it does the second in which the world shifts, embodying a clash of peoples and of civilizations brought into being by dramatic changes in military technology that would cast a wide shadow over the later Middle Ages. Hastings stood not only for the displacement of Anglo-Saxons by Normans, but for the victory of light and mobile Norman knights with couched lances supported by the longer-range weapon of the archers over fixed ax-wielding infantry, a "conflict," in the phrase of historian Lynn White, "between the military methods of the seventh century and those of the eleventh century."[4] The author of the late-eleventh-century *Song of the Battle of Hastings,* Guy of Amiens, tells us that the English, "a race ignorant of war, scorn the solace of horses and trusting in their strength, they stand fast on foot."[5] Panel 144 arrests this transformation in its initial and grandest stage, as the troops in the first line, attached to their horses by stirrups, use the lance as a shock weapon and not a projectile. This shift inaugurates the era of the mounted knight and of a system of land tenure based upon knight's service, the feudalism synonymous with Anglo-Norman society and, indeed, with medieval society in the centuries after the Conquest.

The Tapestry records an instant in time within a world in which images of chronological time and of earthly events were less important than depictions of the defining dramas of biblical history within the scope of Christian providence. Yet this instant is not recorded instantaneously as, say, a painting—or later a photograph—might have captured it in an isolated frame that the viewer could seize with a single look. If ever a work of art defied instantaneous apprehension, it is the Bayeux Tapestry, which by its very length cannot be taken in all at once. The Tapestry covers in its 230 feet the chronological events from Harold's trip to Normandy, which probably took place in the fall of 1064, to the Battle of Hastings two years later.

The Tapestry's temporal dynamism is obvious in the light of comparable scenes from the Harley Psalter, which like the embroidery shows ranks of warriors in battle yet depicts combat as if in a frozen frame (see p. 116). The immobility of the figures of the Psalter is due in part to the fact that we see its pages all at once: The eye is not forced to move from left to right as it does in viewing the Tapestry. Yet it is also a function of the way in which the Tapestry's figures embody the successive stages of the charge of approaching knights, while those of the Harley Psalter, despite their formation in a line, are arrayed randomly with respect to the common maneuver. The comparison is all the more striking when one considers the ease with which action might be rendered via the medium of drawing and wash versus the slowness of embroidery by stem stitch and couched fill.

The moment of contact between the armies of William and Harold is slowed, as in the example we saw earlier of the transmittal of the order of attack (see p. 147). What may have taken a minute or so is dissected into discrete segments depicting the successive split seconds of an event as it unfolds. Yet the Tapestry's rendering of action is odd to the eye and more subtly configured: What appears to be the collective motion of multiple figures is, in fact, one figure engaged in the sequential stages of a single action. The row of knights who one by one hold the lance like a javelin over their head, then move it to a couched position under the arm, are like the individual figures of an animated cartoon, each of which is immobile yet seems to move when displayed with sufficient speed as a series of identical, though slightly altered, images in a flip book.

The stop scroll motion of charging knights is one of the animating principles of the Tapestry, one of the ways in which scenes of movement and of violence come powerfully alive; and it is there almost from the start. As Harold's men board the boat for the ill-fated trip to Normandy in panels 6 and 7, we observe what appear to be five separate figures. Yet each is resolutely engaged in one, and just one, phase of embarkation: The first looks back to the scene of feasting in panel 5 while pointing to the boat, as if he were summoning those still in the hall; the second descends the stairs of the building, holding in his hand a stick that touches the water; the third holds a similar pole, both feet in the water; the fourth holds a dog while wading toward the boat; and the fifth holds a dog in one hand and a falcon in the other, one foot raised from the water as if to step aboard. Each member of the party carries out a separate action in the progression from building to vessel, yielding the impression that every individual figure passes through the actions of the group, which is reassembled in the boat.

In the felling of trees to build the Norman fleet, three woodsmen move through the phases of swinging an ax: The first prepares by drawing it back over his shoulder, the second is in full swing, and the third follows through. In the shooting of the arrow that eventually lands in Harold's eye, eighteen archers in a line enact successively the steps of loading, drawing, raising, and firing a bow.

Great controversy has turned around the relation between

the two figures in panel 169. Some maintain that while the figure on the left with the arrow in his eye under the inscription "Harold has been killed" is indeed Harold, the figure lying on the ground is another knight, possibly even one of Harold's brothers, Leofwine or Gyrth, who have died in panel 151. Though the lack of an arrow in the eye suggests that the second knight is not Harold, the presence of needle holes extending from the nasal guard in a line that crosses the sword lying next to him indicates the original stitching of an arrow in the eye of what in this case is surely the fallen Harold. Recognition of the way the Tapestry Master uses stop scroll motion to portray the movement of a single figure through the *ad seriatim* representation of several figures supports an understanding of two Harolds in the successive stages of dying: Hit by the arrow in the first, he falls to the ground in the second.

The slowing of time, the dissection of time, and the concentration upon the successive instants of a determining historical moment are part of what we might think of as the modernism of the Bayeux Tapestry, which was as startlingly new for its era as, say, Pablo Picasso's *Demoiselles d'Avignon* was for the twentieth century. In its ways of looking back at the events leading to 1066, the Tapestry looks forward to a world in which time is an increasingly secular concept, material objects are interesting in and of themselves, and the rational causes of earthly events outweigh any higher notion of causality. The Tapestry was innovative for its time, and it is still modern in the terms in which we define our own modernity, which explains its enduring appeal.

For a great work of art created in an intensely religious age and with the necessary participation of ecclesiastics, who alone were sufficiently literate to write its inscriptions, the Tapestry is remarkably lacking in religious spirit. Time in the Tapestry is not the *aeternitas* of medieval theologians, for whom earthly events were part of the middle time between the first and second comings of Christ, an anticipation of the final redemption. What we might think of as the narrative economy of the Tapestry—that is, the relation of the time of viewing to the time of events—is uneven. Relatively short time spans sometimes occupy multiple panels, as is the case of the first clash at Hastings, and events of relatively long duration are depicted in a single panel or two, as in the stylized scenes of council, of Edward on his deathbed, or of shipbuilding. The plasticity of time in the Tapestry is synonymous with its secularization, a function of particular activities and occasions and of individual perception. This is one way that we can understand the frequent use of HIC and NUNC ("Here" and "Now") in the inscriptions. The writing in the space between actions and events serves as a constant reminder that the here is now.

Direct references to religion in the Tapestry are few and far between. Harold swears an oath on holy relics, and the very Latin word *sacramentum* betrays its sacred nature. According to chroniclers, William carries the relics hung around his neck into battle along with the papal banner, though both are difficult to locate precisely. Archbishop Odo is a man of God, and he is depicted in the feast before battle in the seat of Christ at the Last Supper. Odo, however, fights as fiercely at Hastings as any other warrior. Archbishop Stigand appears in the orans posture of prayer in panel 72 but plays no larger role in the Tapestry's version of the drama of 1066. The hand of God appears over Westminster Abbey in the scene of Edward's burial, yet Christian providence is balanced by Halley's comet, the "hairy star" seen ominously after Harold's coronation. Numerous chroniclers mention a comet that appeared in February 1066, reached its perihelion on March 27, and attained its maximum brightness in April. Astronomers tell us Halley's comet would have seemed brighter in 1066, when it passed between earth and sun, than in 1985–1986, when it traversed the far side of the sun.

In the absence of emphasis upon religious persons, objects, ritual, or atmosphere, the Tapestry is surprisingly focused upon the things of this world. Its designer is concerned with earthly events, with real places, everyday activities, and even the artisanal crafts of the age. Like the real objects—matchbooks, newspapers, fabric—collated into certain cubist paintings as a defining element of our own modernism for its blurring of the line between life and art, the Tapestry draws upon the images of real events, buildings, and places: Mont-Saint-Michel; the fortresses of Dol, Rennes, and Dinan; Bayeux; Westminster Abbey. One of the reliquaries on which Harold swears contains a named jewel still famous a century later. "The 'eye of the bull,' I have heard it called," observes the poet and chronicler Robert Wace in the *Roman de Rou,* his Old French account of the Scandinavian settlement of Normandy and the Norman invasion of England.

The Tapestry integrates scenes of daily life: seasonal activities like hunting and sowing, but also daily activities like cooking and eating. The stop scroll movement of panels 109–111 shows the successive steps in the preparation of spits and skewers of meat and of bread as they pass from fire and oven to table. This scene of feasting before the Battle of Hastings is remarkable in the attention to detail, to the tools used in the cooking and handling of food: the shape of the mechanism turning the spit, the lineup of skewers, the tongs with which bread is lifted, and the shape of the sideboard improvised from shields on which the food is laid on plates and bowls. A close look at panels 110–111 reveals six figures: The first holds spits of meat in his right hand, while handing the spits of meat in his left hand to the second figure, who receives spits in his left hand while passing skewers with whole chickens through a doorway to the third figure, who receives them with his right hand and holds a bowl with a long-handled spoon with his left hand. Between the bowls and plates lie several cleavers or hacking knives. The fourth figure has placed his left hand on a bowl while he passes something not quite visible in the direction of the fifth figure, who blows a horn to announce dinner. To his left, a figure with a twisted body looks back at the scene of food preparation upon the sideboard while clearly moving into the space of eating. A figure kneels in the open space of the hemicyclical dining table, a towel draped over one arm, as he places a large bowl before the diners. Bowls, plates, knives, and fish lie upon the table at which are seated six figures whose own bodily postures and gestures, in particular the raised pointing left arm of the fifth in the series, move us across the scene of supper and into the succeeding interior space of the war room, where William orders trenches to be dug at Hastings. In what is an extraordinarily smooth transition from kitchen to council, involving as it does some sixteen human figures and focusing upon the implements and activities of the cooking, preparation, and eating of food, the Tapestry Master offers as good a glimpse at the everyday life of eleventh-century knights as can be found.

With similar interest and attention to detail, the Tapestry shows the stages of fleet building in panels 81–84, the felling of trees, the shaping and shaving of lumber, the joining of planks, the launching, mooring, and loading of boats. Amid the four carpenters wielding hammers and carving tools stands a shipwright directing the others, as indicated by an arm raised in the gesture, used throughout the Tapestry, of command. In the upper boat of main panel 84, one of the shipbuilders holds what looks like a measuring device in his two hands. From the scene of shipbuilding, four men standing in the water launch the boats while a fifth attaches the ropes to a mooring post in a series of stop scroll motions in which the objects from panel 85 are literally pulled across the Tapestry into panel 86.

The loading of the boats in panels 88–90 is remarkably precise in the display of the embarkation of the weapons and victuals of war. Nine figures bear full coats of mail suspended on poles, helmets, bundles of swords, an ax, and a lance, while two others tow a cart on which sit a keg of wine, five helmets, and twenty arrows pointing upward and set in a vertical rack. Between them men carry on their shoulders smaller containers of liquid, a slender barrel and a bladder, as well as a sack of grain. In panel 102, the Tapestry shows the unloading of horses, an innovative technical feat unknown to the Normans of Normandy before 1066 and to which we shall return in the discussion of the strategic contributions to the Conquest made by the Normans from the Mediterranean and Middle East.

The Tapestry Master is interested in the particularity and the working of things, in the division of tasks that go into a common enterprise, in the ways that men make, shape, and consume everyday goods as well as the special staples of war. He is a stickler for details—the mustache that distinguishes Anglo-Saxons from Normans, the tunics lifted as men step into the water at Bosham, the plumb line dropped from a boat in Harold's landing on the Norman coast, the weather vane placed atop Westminster Abbey, the carved dragons on the prow and stern of warships, the stone dropped by one worker on the head of another in building the fortifications at Hastings, the harness, saddlery, and even the sexual excitement of horses. One of the steeds held by Turold in panel 24, the horse on which Harold arrives at William's palace in panel 34, Harold's mount upon return to England in panel 63, and William's charger brought to him by the reins in panel 121 are all depicted in an impressive state of equine erection.

In the presentation of the political happenings of a two-year period and the one-day battle that displaced the leaders of a population and changed the nature of the known world, the Tapestry Master sews as seamless a transition from one scene to the next as can be imagined. He is interested in the working of things, and the eye of the viewer often lingers over details or is distracted by the decorative figures and fables in the margins. Yet the smooth progress of history drawn as a linear progression from one scene to the next renders a world in which events—from beginning to end—seem inevitable. The Tapestry Master shows astonishing skill in linking the discrete events of the embroidery and in keeping its action moving from left to right, and this via the attuned crafting of trees, architecture, and the human body.

The odd stylized trees of the Tapestry are a transitional device, marking geographical space, indicating departure, arrival, or a change of direction. Trees signal Harold's arrival in Bosham in panel 4 and in panel 16 link Guy of Ponthieu's capture of Harold to their departure in the direction of Guy's castle at Beaurain. This second example is interesting because the horses and men to the left of the tree face left, and those on the right face right, the exception being the dogs on the left who have already begun to run toward Beaurain. The tree serves as a means of illustrating the action of turning around, and its interlaced branches, which cross one another before fanning in the direction opposite their rooting in the trunk, make the visual bond.

The crosshatched tree along the Norman coast is a link between scenes, as is the tree of panel 21, whose branches weave together the spy behind a pillar of Guy of Ponthieu's council chamber and the shoulders of Guy's men receiving messengers from William in panel 22. A similar effect is produced by the tree that makes the transition between William's messengers riding to the left and the arrival of the news of Harold's capture. A lookout who has climbed this tree in panel 27 balances the branches facing the scene of William's court. A reversal of direction at the point of Harold's arrival at Rouen is marked by two trees whose entwined branches point both left and right. Bidirectional interlaced trees stand at the departure and arrival scenes of the news of Harold's usurpation on both sides of the Channel in panels 76 and 79. Three such trees signal a shift in direction and the beginning of battle in panel 122, and a similar trio separates Norman and Anglo-Saxon scouts in panel 131.

The Tapestry's trees are not three-dimensional, as in nature. They are flat and are woven as if their branches were made of single strands of enlarged thread frayed at the end by leafy tendrils. Pointing right and left, they bind the scenes on either side and thus keep the figures moving through complicated itineraries, like that of William's messengers who ride from Rouen to Beaurain and back, and through discrete physical spaces, like the inside and outside of Guy's and William's castles, in smooth transition from left to right across the breadth of the embroidery.

Architecture in the Tapestry has a similar function, the joining of buildings marking a movement from one interior space to the next and thus a progression through time. This is true, for example, of the buildings beginning in the scene of Harold's interview with King Edward upon his return from Normandy in panel 65 and ending with the far end of Westminster Abbey in the scene of Edward's burial. The room in which Harold stands before the seated Edward is bounded on the left by a tower with circular staircase, windows, and turret and on the right by a similar tower, which is itself attached by a sloping roof to a shorter tower that forms one side of the inclined roof, on which stands the man placing the weathercock atop Westminster Abbey, linked to the original interior by a series of connected towers and roofs. The same is true of the building in which Harold is crowned, the first in a series of three rooms separated by turrets with doors and roofs in which Harold's counselors look back at the new king and then forward in the direction of Halley's comet.

The human bodies that inhabit and move through the buildings of the Tapestry work sculpturally to keep things moving. Figures on one side of a crowd scene might be planted in one space, while those on the other side move toward another. Individual bodies are sometimes twisted so as to indicate motion from left to right. The figure leaving Harold's hall at Bosham faces back to the room while his left foot and arm are turned toward those already engaged in boarding the boat to Normandy. The same is true in panel 20 of the spy, whose right side of the body and right ear are turned attentively to the happenings at Guy of Ponthieu's court in Beaurain yet whose foot, planted on the other side of the pillar behind which he hides, is turned in the direction of where such news might be transmitted. One of Harold's men, who observes him swear on relics, has one foot planted on land and turned toward the water that will carry him back to England, while a second knight, whose right leg crosses the first knight's left leg, is turned bodily toward the water in which he stands. It is as if they are in two scenes, interior and travel, at once.

Of the eleven courtiers who stand in two rooms after Harold's coronation, those on the left face toward the new king and Stigand, while those on the right are turned progressively toward the appearance of Halley's comet. In the scene of the issuing of the command to build the invasion fleet, the woodsman in panel 80 listens with his head turned to William and Odo, while his body—both feet, both arms, and ax—seems already to have left the room in execution of the ducal order. The knight in panel 135 turns his head toward William, delivering the command of attack, while his mounted body rides forward into battle. In panels 154–156, the twisted bodies of horses connect the scenes of chaotic battle to the left and right. The William of panel 160, rumored to have been killed, turns his raised visor to look back, showing those behind him that he is still alive, while riding forward above the very place in the Tapestry where archers begin to load the arrows that will end the fight.

A remarkable variant of the bodies twisted between scenes lies in the bodies with distended necks depicted within tableaux. The courtiers in Harold's interview with Guy of Ponthieu extend their necks to the right, while the spy behind a pillar stretches his to the left in a gesture meant to transmit the idea of attentive listening. Those surrounding the Norman throne in panel 37 crane their necks to take in the exchange between the captured Harold and William. The same is true of those in panel 59, where Harold swears his oath on relics. The Harold in panel 64, newly returned from Normandy and standing before the ailing king Edward, exhibits what is perhaps the longest neck in Western art. The Tapestry Master might have intended Harold's long neck to emphasize the bowed head acknowledging guilt atop a shrinking body. This is, after all, a world in which inner states are revealed primarily through external gestures and bodily signs. Edward, whose own strained neck may be a sign of his failing health and weariness, points the long finger of admonishment—in fact, one of the longest fingers in Western art—at the cringing Harold.

Long fingers and craning necks are characteristic of the Winchester style of illuminated manuscripts found in and around Canterbury both before and after the Conquest (see p. 115). They are an integral part of Anglo-Saxon representations of the body, just as the hip-shot women, whose hips sway so severely as to appear out of joint, are a part of Gothic painting and sculpture. Yet the dislocated finger and the "wrung neck" style of the Tapestry is neither just a borrowing from elsewhere nor a consistent means of representing the body. On the contrary, the strained necks of courtiers and kings appear exclusively among the standing figures in fixed portrayals of council, in scenes, in other words, in which physical movement is reduced to a minimum and action consists primarily of conversation. Like the twisted bodies turning between preceding and succeeding tableaux and thus linking one scene to the next, the wrung necks motivate time within a tableau. They are a means of keeping time moving at those moments of verbal exchange when, visually speaking, time slows down and, as we have seen, even the inscriptions are mute. The "wrung neck" style flattens the visual axis along which the eye moves and thus preserves forward motion in the telling of the Conquest story.

A similar technique is found in the overlapping of figural planes within and between tableaux. In the depiction of shields, boats, horses, and mounted knights, the right part of the object on the left lies regularly over the left part of that to its immediate right. The shields lining the gunwales of Harold's boats traveling to Normandy and returning to England, like the shields lining the gunwales of William's fleet crossing the Channel, so consistently protrude over one another from left to right that they resemble the bristly scales of an echinodermal fish. The layering of the boats of William's fleet mirrors the shields along their upper edges: Boats to the left overlap those to the right. The horses and riders who cross the river Couesnon at the beginning of the Breton campaign partially cover one another from left to right, as do those who participate in the first clash, beginning with William's order of attack, through the meeting of the wall of Anglo-Saxon shields, which are themselves overlaid, left over right. Despite the chaos of battle, the knights who mount the final attack remain faithful to this important visual rule of the Tapestry's means of recounting a great military victory: Figures on the left partially cover those to their immediate right.

Consistent overlapping of perspectival planes is not a function of the making of the Tapestry. Embroidery from left to right would have produced, in the arrangement of stem and laid couch stitches, just the opposite—a layering such that the threads sewn progressively to the right covered those to their left. The counterlayering of shields, boats, and knights is another of the techniques the Tapestry Master uses to maintain movement of the eye from left to right, rendering the impression that history itself has but one direction, and that direction aligns with the well-known outcome of the events leading to victory. Movement backward would be against the Tapestry's visual grain.

Here we find ourselves before one of those moments at which the form of an art object and its meaning coincide. The overlapping of planes in scenes of movement, the extension of necks in stationary sets, the presentation of faces in some degree of profile, and the twisting of bodies between tableaux all contribute to a flattening of history along a horizontal plane. The actions and events of the Tapestry are so smoothly intertwined that, as in the thrusting, forward-moving technique of stop scroll motion, the end of history seems inevitable. How different the unidirectional nature of the Tapestry is, for example, from the repeat patterns of Byzantine silks, in which the pleasure of decorative design removes the eye from time and from the urgency of a story. Or how different from the disposition of a tympanum over the portal of a Romanesque or Gothic church, in which Christ sits in the middle of the figures to his left and right in the sculptural depiction of some future moment of final redemption outside historical time. The symmetrical design of both silk and tympanum could not be further from the Tapestry's impatient movement along the flattened axis of human history, from left to right, and from the beginning of the events in and around the English succession to their visual, chronological, and unavoidable end.

In the masterful visual and dramatic presentation of the events leading to the Norman Conquest of 1066 as if they were inescapable, the Tapestry most resembles the great victory friezes of late antiquity—the Column of Trajan, which commemorates the emperor's successful campaign in Dacia (113), and that of Marcus Aurelius (180), both still standing in Rome. Like the Tapestry, Trajan's Column contains set motifs not only of battle, but of the transportation by ship of troops and equipment, marches through enemy territory and encampment, council in which the emperor is seated among his advisers, negotiation, reconnaissance, rallying of troops, and equestrian charge. Certain scenes of the Tapestry resemble those of Roman victory columns even more precisely. The Dacians on Trajan's Column cross a marsh just as William, Harold, and their men cross the river Couesnon; Roman woodsmen fell trees for fortification just as William's woodsmen cut timber for construction of the Norman fleet; Roman soldiers build castles in scene LXVIII of the column in a fashion somewhat like that of the laborers crossing spades in the fortification of Hastings in the Tapestry. The most avid proponent of the direct influence of classical victory columns upon the Tapestry Master, O. K. Werckmeister, sees in the three-arched, gabled porch at the right end of the stretch of water into which the finished Norman vessels are being pulled in panel 87 a version of a structure in embarkation scene XXXIII of Trajan's Column.[6] The mother fleeing with her child by the hand from an English house torched by Norman pillagers in panel 118 closely resembles the mother and child in scene XX on the Column of Marcus Aurelius.

Scholars have wondered from the start if the Tapestry Master could have drawn not only set motifs and particular images, but the very concept of "continuous pictorial narrative" from the monumental victory friezes of Rome, either directly or via some intermediary.

The case for direct contact is sustained by the fact that despite the height of Trajan's Column, which renders its uppermost parts inaccessible to the eye of a viewer on the ground, all but one of the motifs that reappear in the Tapestry are located in the lowermost third of its one hundred feet. In the tenth and eleventh centuries, Anglo-Saxons as well as Normans were regular visitors to Rome, often on the way to or from the Holy Land. Harold's brother Tostig, slain by Harold at the Battle of Stamford Bridge, accompanied their brother Gyrth, who died with Harold at Hastings, to Rome in 1061. The Anglo-Saxons maintained an ec-

Woman and child fleeing, Column of Marcus Aurelius, Rome

© ALINARI/ART RESOURCE, N.Y.

clesiastical community in Rome, and the last Anglo-Saxon abbot of Saint Augustine's Abbey, Canterbury, traveled to the Holy City. His replacement, Abbot Scotland; Bishop Geoffrey of Coutances, who took part in the Norman Conquest; and William's archbishop of Canterbury, Lanfranc, had all been to Rome. Before undertaking the invasion of England, William sought the blessing of Pope Alexander II, who gave him a banner "as a token of kingship," though he was not yet king. The pope, as we shall see, relied upon protection from Normans not only in the Holy City, but throughout the Mediterranean. Odo maintained a palace in Rome until his disgrace in 1082. Normans rescued the pope from imprisonment when Germans sacked Rome in 1084. There was, in other words, plenty of opportunity for either Anglo-Saxons or Normans to have seen Trajan's Column or that of Marcus Aurelius before the Tapestry was embroidered.

The image of woodsmen felling trees in the Anglo-Saxon manuscript calendar month of July is close enough to the images of woodcutting both on Trajan's Column and on the Tapestry for it to serve as an example of how a single motif might have been transported from Rome to England (see p. 114). A potential route of transmission lies among the Germanic rulers to the East. Partisans still of Charlemagne's dream of restoring empire, the Ottonian emperors were frequent visitors to Rome. Sometime between 1015 and 1022, Saint Bernward of Hildesheim, who had lived with his pupil Otto III on the Aventine in Rome, ordered a twelve-foot-high Christian version of Trajan's Column. The eight spirals of Bernward's Column, representing the life of Jesus along with his triumphant entry into Jerusalem, still stand in the east choir of the Church of Saint Michael, Hildesheim. (Harvard University's Busch-Reisinger Museum owns a full-scale reproduction.) We have seen that the Tapestry Master turned to Byzantine, Roman, and Ottonian imperial models in the representation of frontal Harold, and it is possible that the very idea of a scrolling monumental victory narrative arrived in England or France via the Ottonian heirs to Rome, whom the Normans, in a medieval version of manifest destiny, sought in their turn to replace.

The Tapestry's insistent movement from left to right coincides with the movement of history from east to west, of which the Norman Conquest represents an important stage. The Conquest represents the ultimate step in a career: "A king obtained a kingdom, a duke a dukedom, / and so he obtained the title of Caesar. / He alone, while he lived, ruled a double office / and was more exalted than all caesars and dukes"—so exclaims Baudri de Bourgueil in a poem addressed to William the Conqueror's daughter

Adela (v. 555). And it represents the ultimate stage in the unfolding of history. For William's biographer William of Poitiers, Caesar's invasions of England from Gaul in 55 and 54 B.C. are exemplary events in the planning of William's crossing of the Channel. "Who could hope that within the prescribed space of one year a fleet could be built, or that oarsmen could be found to man it when it was built?" he asks. "Who would not fear that this new expedition would reduce the prosperous condition of their native land to utter wretchedness? Who would not affirm that the resources of a Roman emperor would be unequal to such a difficult enterprise?" Yet for William of Poitiers, the example of Rome is not rooted in a sufficiently distant past. He compares Duke William's avenging of the wrong done him by Harold to Agamemnon of the house of Atreus, who "went to avenge the violation of his brother's bed with a thousand ships." "Greece also tells the story," writes William of Poitiers, "of how Xerxes joined the towns of Sestos and Abydos, separated by the sea, with a bridge of boats. As for us we proclaim in truth that William linked together by his sway the wide extent of the Norman and English lands."

William's biographer hitches him to the glory of Greece and of Persia. The Persian Xerxes I, having placed a bridge of boats across the strait of Hellespont, was defeated by the Greeks at Salamis in 480 B.C. For William of Poitiers, the courage that Duke William shows in ordering a copious breakfast on the morning of the Channel crossing, despite the failure to locate the rest of his fleet, makes him the equal of Aeneas, whose destiny took him from the flames of Troy to Italy and whose descendants were the founders of Rome. "Virgil, the prince of poets, would not have thought it unfitting," William of Poitiers observes, "to insert in his praise of the Trojan Aeneas (who was the ancestor and glory of ancient Rome) an account of the confidence and purpose of this banquet." William the Conqueror, he assures us, "so surpassed" even the bravest of his army "in courage as well as in wisdom that he deserves to be placed above certain of the ancient generals of the Greeks and Romans.... Against Harold, who was such a man as poems liken to Hector or Turnus, William would have dared to fight in single combat no less than Achilles against Hector, or Aeneas against Turnus."

Passing through Rome, the lineage from ancient Greece to England is unbroken. The twelfth-century historian Geoffrey of Monmouth derives the name "Britain" from Aeneas's grandson Brutus, who left Rome to found a new Troy in England, which was until that time called Albion. Geoffrey's Latin *History of the Kings of Britain* was translated into Anglo-Norman French by Robert Wace, who in the *Roman de Rou* insists that the Norman charge up the hill at Senlac is led by the "gonfanon that came from Rome." As a later rendering of the Trojan War, the Norman Conquest of England fulfills the manifest destiny of the Normans, whose legitimate patrimony stretches from Achilles to Aeneas, to William, and from Greece to Rome, Rome to Rouen, and Rouen to London.

The Bayeux Tapestry is a Janus-faced work. Looking back to Rome and the triumphal columns associated with Roman conquest, its own ways of presenting history and the history it presents make a powerful statement of Norman ambitions in the wider world. The Tapestry adapts a local artistic medium— Anglo-Saxon embroidery—to a classical form: the victory frieze. Understood in this light, the Tapestry both contains the image of the papal banner from Rome and is a long banner pointing back to Rome—more precisely, to the combined operations of Normans and the pope in the decades before the Conquest of 1066 and culminating in the First Crusade of 1096–1098.

Scandinavians from the North, like Harald Hardråda, were not the only travelers to the Middle East, nor was Byzantium the only

destination. Those who had settled in Normandy also maintained contact with visitors from the East. Richard II (ruled
996–1026), William the Conqueror's grandfather, received at
his ducal seat in Rouen monks from Mount Sinai, upon whom he
bestowed generous gifts. Richard's son Duke Robert the Magnif-
icent (ruled 1027–1035) died while on a pilgrimage to Jerusalem
via Constantinople, where he had mixed dealings with Emperor
Michael IV. Leaving young William to deal with his obstreperous
barons, Robert was first buried in Nicaea. The twelfth-century
historian William of Malmesbury tells us that William dispatched a messenger to bring his father's bones back to Normandy when the Turks captured Nicaea in 1086, but the
returning messenger, upon learning of William's death in 1087,
had Robert I reinterred among the Normans of Apulia.

Many Normans, whose northern ancestors had settled along
the coast and riverways of northwestern France in the tenth century, had by the 1130s found Normandy too small, so they left to
seek their fortunes in the South. According to Amatus of Montecassino, whose *History of the Normans* recounts Norman exploits in
the Mediterranean, the first Normans to intervene in the
Mediterranean were pilgrims coming back from Jerusalem in
999—"before a thousand years after Christ," in Amatus's phrase.
Stopping in Salerno, under siege by Arabs from Sicily, they bor-
rowed arms and liberated the city, whose inhabitants "thanked
them greatly, offered them gifts, promised them great rewards,
and entreated the Normans to stay." Though the pilgrims de-
clined, they returned to Normandy with gifts of "citrus fruit, al-
monds, preserved nuts, purple cloth, and instruments of iron
adorned with gold to induce the Normans to come to the land of
milk and honey and of so many beautiful things."[7]

The Mediterranean was ripe for the intervention of newcom-
ers. Native Latins or Italians, the papacy, Greeks or Byzantines,
and Saracens or Arabs had fought for centuries among themselves to control "the land of milk and honey and of so many

beautiful things." All were in search of mercenaries to help settle old territorial disputes. The Greeks already employed Scandinavians, sometimes even against the Normans of Normandy who had resettled in the South, though the more southern Normans had ambitions upon Byzantium itself, the more the Eastern emperors turned to Anglo-Saxons for protection.

The first Norman to gain noble title in the Mediterranean was Count Rainolf, who in 1029 received the town and territory of Aversa along with the hand of the sister of the Duke of Naples. A Norman contingent participated in the reconquest of Sicily under the Byzantine general George Maniakès in 1038–1040. Among these were two sons of Tancred of Hauteville. Tancred was a knight and landholder of moderate means, yet his Norman patrimony in the region known as the Cotentin was insufficient. Eight of his twelve sons went abroad, and eventually Apulia, Calabria, and Sicily would be theirs.

In 1053, a united Norman force defeated the papal army at Civitate as Pope Leo IX looked on from the ramparts of the city. Civitate marked the beginning of the Norman military miracle. The confrontation between the old Germanic tactics of the pope's Swabian elite, with their two-handed swords, and lance-wielding Norman knights on horseback was a preview of Hastings, where the Norman light cavalry would thirteen years later defeat the Anglo-Saxons and their Danish "bearded axes." It also marked the beginning of the alliance between the Normans and the papacy, which chose to ally with those it could not defeat. In the late 1050s, Pope Nicholas II invested Robert Guiscard, son of Tancred of Hauteville, as Duke of Apulia and Calabria, and Richard of Aversa, son of Rainolf, as Prince of Capua. Together they joined the pope's campaign to recapture Italy and Sicily from the Byzantines and the Saracens. Bari fell in 1072, Salerno in 1076, Benevento and Naples in 1077. The Normans took possession of northern Sicily, Palermo, in 1072. By 1080—that is, just about the time of the embroidery of the Bayeux Tapestry—the Normans controlled all of southern Italy and a large part of Sicily as well. Even before Pope Alexander II sent a banner to William to carry with him in crossing the English Channel, he invested Roger of Hauteville, Robert's younger brother, with a papal banner and absolution for all who fought with him against the heathen. Roger, the eighth and youngest Hauteville, became Count of Sicily in 1072.

A few Norman travelers made it as far as Constantinople. According to the churchman Adémar de Chabannes (989–1034), a group of pilgrims who left France in 1026 celebrated mass in Hagia Sophia. Ivo of Bellême, bishop of the Norman diocese of Séez, undertook a voyage of penance to southern Italy and Constantinople, imposed upon him by Pope Leo IX at the Council of Reims in 1049 for having burned down the Church of Saint Gervaise at Séez. While in the Mediterranean, he solicited pious gifts from former parishioners. Geoffrey of Montbray, bishop of Coutances in Normandy, went around 1050 to Apulia and Calabria to visit a former member of his diocese, Robert Guiscard. He returned, in the phrase of his biographer, "with lots of gold and silver, precious stones and luxurious cloths as well as other rich gifts . . . with which he enriched his church both inside and out." In 1066, Geoffrey of Montbray crossed the Channel with Duke William.

The Normans of Normandy remained in contact with their southern brothers and cousins, and some returned to participate in the Conquest. Guy of Amiens, author of *The Song of the Battle of Hastings,* mentions that men from Apulia, Calabria, and Sicily joined William's invasion force. And the anonymous author of *The Song of Roland,* composed in or around 1098 and imbued with the spirit of the First Crusade in its glorification of Charlemagne's campaign in Spain in 778, makes what appears to be a slip in his catalog of the emperor's exploits:

An amazing man, Charles!
conquered Apulia, conquered all of Calabria,
crossed the salt sea on his way into England,
won its tribute, got Peter's pence for Rome. (v. 371–374)

Eighth-century Franks never captured Apulia (Puglia) or Calabria, nor did they cross "the salt sea" to recover "Peter's pence for Rome." But the Normans did, and one of the explicit goals of the Norman Conquest was to bring the Church of England, which had strayed in the appointment of Stigand as archbishop of Canterbury, within the Roman Pale.

The Italian and Sicilian Normans who responded to William's call for troops contributed to the Conquest a knowledge of warfare that they had gained and tested in the Mediterranean. Hugh of Grantmesnil, who came from a modest aristocratic family that came to power under William's grandfather Duke Richard II, had fought in the South with the sons of Tancred of Hauteville. Hugh was with William at the Councils of Bonneville-sur-Toques and Lillebonne, where the invasion of England was planned, and as we know from Robert Wace's *Roman de Rou,* he narrowly escaped death at Hastings. The Normans who had fought in the South brought back not only the experience of use of light cavalry and the couched lance as a shock weapon, tested at Civitate in 1053, but methods of encampment dating back to Roman military tactics. The writings of Caesar and Vegetius were still known to educated men of William's court. Normans of the eleventh century turned to the Roman example of a successful crossing of the English Channel, just as Napoleon and Hitler turned, in nourishing their own designs upon England, to the Norman Conquest and its embodiment in the Bayeux Tapestry.

Before 1066, Duke William had been used to military incursions no larger than the raids, sieges, and short decisive battles by which he managed, beginning at the age of nineteen or twenty, when he defeated rebellious barons at Val-ès-Dunes (1047) to his defeat of the French king and the Count of Anjou (1057), to secure the duchy of Normandy under his command. We have some idea of what William's early military career might have been like via the Tapestry's depiction of the excursion to Brittany and the attacks on Dol, Rennes, and Dinan.

The invasion of England, however, was an undertaking of a wholly different magnitude. It is estimated that the building of a fleet of 700 ships in three months would have taken 40,000 to 50,000 trees and occupied the labor of some 8,400 workmen, though it is assumed that William requisitioned as many existing vessels as possible in order to spare just such an expenditure. If 8,000 troops fought at Hastings, it is reckoned that another 6,000 men were at the garrison at Dives-sur-Mer in roles of support—cooks, carpenters, smiths, priests—as well as the ship crews dedicated to the actual transport. The encampment of 14,000 men and 2,000–3,000 horses represented supply and waste problems of staggering proportions, given, by the calculation of Bernard Bachrach, that each 1,500-pound horse produced 65–70 pounds of feces and 8–8.5 gallons of urine each day, for a monumental total of 5 million pounds of feces and 700,000 gallons of urine during the month at Dives-sur-Mer—this in addition to the estimated 450 tons of human feces that had to be carted away.[8]

The organization that went into an encampment of this complexity and size in all likelihood came to Normandy from the Mediterranean with the Normans who had served abroad—whether in southern Italy, Sicily, or Byzantium—and who had gained in their time there knowledge of Greek methods of encampment and naval transport. The Byzantines developed signaling systems for night navigation and a protocol of "deep-sea harbor" using deep-sea anchor and windlass to prevent the very scattering of the fleet that William experienced on the night of September 27, 1066. In *The Song of Roland*, the troops who come to help the Saracens of Spain from the port of Alexandria set sail at night:

> Great are the hosts of that enemy race
> They steer ever onward, by sail, by oar.
> Atop the masts on the ships' high prows
> carbuncles shine, lanterns on lanterns shine,
> and cast forth from on high such blazing light!
> the sea is fairer for it, in the dark night;
> and as they come upon the land of Spain,
> All that country glows with that pagan light. (v. 2,630)

The Byzantines were organized into three-hundred-man field command units based on ten-man groups, and the three hundred Normans who participated in the invasion of Sicily in 1038 could easily have learned about such a system from their Byzantine commanding general George Maniakès, as could the three hundred Norman horsemen who in 1041 served under Arduin, the *topoterites* of Melfi.

The transport of horses as depicted in the Tapestry is a remarkable accomplishment. Neither the Vikings nor the English took horses with them in crossing large bodies of water for the purpose of fighting but relied instead on the capture of mounts upon landing for attack. The transport of horses as part of William's invasion fleet shows a commitment and an immediate preparedness to fight on horseback with lance, since the Normans depended on mounts trained in the maneuvers of thrusting and fitted with stirrups to hold the mounted knight in place.

The hauling of horses was practiced among the Greeks and Arabs, as it had been by the Romans who participated in Caesar's crossings from Gaul to Britain in the first century B.C. The

Byzantines had specially designed ships—*hippagogoi*—to carry horses, and records show that in the tenth century they transported over four thousand men and mounts in operations against Crete and Sicily. Normans participated in the Byzantine ferrying of horses to Sicily in 1038; and in 1061, Robert Guiscard sent some three hundred horsemen across the Strait of Messina. Between 1060 and 1064, Normans launched no fewer than eight expeditions to Sicily accompanied by horse. The building of ships suitable for horse transport was a skill practiced in the Mediterranean ports of Pisa, Gaeta, Naples, Amalfi, and Sorrento. As Baudri of Bourgueil tells us, in the preparation of 1066, native Normans were not the only shipwrights, but "carpenters were summoned from all over the world and turned from building houses to building ships."

In the decades following the Conquest, some Normans from southern Italy and Sicily who had not joined William entered the service of the Byzantine emperor, where they encountered the descendants of their Scandinavian ancestors, who had come to Constantinople directly from the North without passing through Normandy. Arriving in groups of several hundred under the command of leaders who had tested their mettle against the Saracens in Sicily or Calabria, Italian Normans aided the emperor in his struggle against the Turks of Central Asia. Some of the names of individual mercenaries are known. Roussel de Bailleul came to Apulia with Robert Guiscard, fought alongside his brother Roger against the Saracens around 1069, then passed to the East into the service of the emperor. He fought with Emperor Romanus IV (Diogenes) against Sultan Alp Arslan in 1071 as well as with Emperor Michael Doukas and the young Isaac Comnenus against the Turks in 1073. Leaving imperial service and living the life of an adventurer and freebooter, Roussel was eventually captured by the future emperor Alexius I Comnenus, imprisoned, and released, only to become head of the Varangians before his death in 1078.

While some of the Normans of Italy fought for the emperor of Byzantium, others wanted to be emperor. After his investiture by the pope, Robert Guiscard considered himself to be the successor upon Italian soil of the basileus, the Eastern emperor, who had once ruled Apulia and Calabria. Having amassed much territory in Italy, Guiscard dreamed of conquering Byzantium as well. The Byzantines continued to support revolts against him, and he had concluded a peace by accepting a marriage alliance in 1074 between Constantine, the son of Emperor Michael VII Doukas, and his daughter, who was sent to Constantinople, where she entered the imperial *gynecaeum* and took the Greek name Helen. The fall of Michael in 1078 furnished a pretext for invasion, which was prepared in 1080 and 1081.

To Robert Guiscard, the only safety lay in conquering Greece itself. His forces reached Avlona and Corfu, which he captured, then turned to Durazzo, where Mediterranean Normans fought against English troops in the service of Alexius Comnenus— some of the very Anglo-Saxons, in fact, who had left England with Sigurd and had remained in Constantinople instead of heading with their fellow exiles to New England in the Crimea (see pp. 164–65). Guiscard was deterred from moving on to Constantinople only by a rebellion at home in Apulia, fomented by Comnenus.

After Durazzo, Pope Gregory wrote to Robert Guiscard to congratulate him on his victory against a Byzantine army, saying that he saw in his success "a token of St. Peter's patronage and a promise of greater things to come." The events of 1081 and 1082 in the Mediterranean took place only sixteen years after the Norman Conquest, in the very window during which the Bayeux Tapestry was probably embroidered. The "promise of greater things to come" would, of course, occur some sixteen years later, when the Normans of England and Normandy would join the Normans of Italy in the undertaking of the First Crusade, which many consider a second Norman Conquest.

William the Conqueror nourished imperial ambitions from the start of his rule over both Normandy and England, and such ambitions were inflected by a long view toward Byzantium. William had himself crowned in the Byzantine style—that is to say, by acclamation—and on Christmas Day 1066. The choice of date is significant, selected as it was in the line of Frankish, Ottonian, and Byzantine emperors who had themselves crowned on December 25—Charlemagne in 800, Otto II in 967, Otto III in 983, Henry III in 1046, and the Byzantine Michael II in 820. William's steward before the Conquest, Odo of Mézidon, had spent three years in Constantinople, where he commanded a squadron of mercenaries. He spoke Greek and was present at the coronation ceremony of Constantine X Doukas on December 25, 1059. William's crown, according to Guy of Amiens, author of *The Song of the Battle of Hastings,* was Greek in design: "He commanded that a noble crown of gold and jewels, such as would be seemly, be fashioned for him by a master-craftsman. Arabia provided gold, Nilus gems from the river; Greece inspired a smith skilled in the art as he who—scarcely inferior to Solomon—created Solomon's wondrous and befitting diadem."

In the imperial style of Byzantium, adopted in the West after the marriage of the emperor's daughter Theophanou to Otto II, William wanted to have his wife crowned alongside him. However, according to William's biographer William of Poitiers, Mathilda was still in Normandy, and his councillors convinced him to proceed with the coronation as soon as possible. Queen by title on December 25, 1066, Mathilda was not crowned in England until Easter 1068.

The coins struck by William after the Norman Conquest were of the Byzantine style, showing the ruler full frontal, sword drawn and held conspicuously in front of the face, such as can be seen on Continental coins that imitate the Greek, but especially on the coins minted by Emperor Isaac Comnenus (ruled 1057–1059). It is entirely possible that the Normans who had served at the imperial court in the East and were paid in such a coin type introduced them to the duchy. The similarity of both the drawn-sword coins of Isaac Comnenus and of William to representations of William in the Bayeux Tapestry, such as that in panel 58, where he observes Harold swear his oath on relics, is striking and significant. William's seal, like his coins, combines the Byzantine sword-type frontal pose and cruciform orb.

William in the posture and holding the attributes of Byzantine imperial power is a lesson in what the historian Peter Brown terms "cultural hydraulics" in describing the movement of ideas and images from the East to the West. In the centuries before the Conquest, men and ideas, men and goods, gold and coins, precious objects of all sorts, furs and clothes, manuscripts, and decorative textiles were readily transportable. They circulated via artists who emigrated, as many Greek artists did, as refugees during the iconoclast period of the tenth century, in which they were forced to find work abroad; or via artists who traveled west with diplomatic or trade embassies. Art objects circulated via pilgrims to the Middle East. They circulated as a result of gift, purchase, commission,

Sword-type seal of William the Conqueror

© BRITISH LIBRARY/HIP/ART RESOURCE, N.Y.

and plunder. And when they circulated, they bore with them not only the ideas contained in the books of late antiquity, but motifs and designs that captivated the eye, that reappeared in the art of the Scandinavians and the Anglo-Saxons, and that are, as we have seen throughout, an integral part of the Bayeux Tapestry.

William in the mode of a sword-type coin, frontal Harold in majesty, Edward in dormition upon his deathbed, the fables, exotic paired animals, spiraliform, and foliate decorations of the borders are all images that reached the Tapestry Master from afar. Though they may have passed through other cultures—Ottonian, Salian, Roman, Scandinavian, Norman, and Anglo-Saxon—on their way either to England or France, they are nonetheless distant visitors from the East. The liveliness of contact among the Scandinavian, Norman, and Anglo-Saxon worlds and the Mediterranean means that the inclusion in the Bayeux Tapestry of material so charged with cultural meaning is both intentional and strategic. The orientalism of the Tapestry is not dead metaphor, but a living eye turned, at a point exactly equidistant between the Norman Conquest of 1066 and the First Crusade of 1098, toward the Middle East.

William ruled for twenty-one years after the Conquest and died in 1087, but his family along with Normans from Normandy as well as the Mediterranean responded to Pope Urban II's call on November 27, 1095, for "liberation of the East, the Eastern Churches and the Holy Places from oppression and defilement by Unbelievers." The precipitating event was the growing strength of the Seldjuk Turks, who menaced Christians in the East and cut off pilgrimage routes through Asia Minor, provoking an appeal for military assistance by Emperor Alexius Comnenus, who feared that not even the imperial city was safe. The armies of the West were to assemble in Constantinople before heading to Jerusalem.

Among the knights setting out for the Middle East were William's oldest son, Robert "Curthose," Duke of Normandy; his son-in-law Count Stephen of Blois; his nephew by marriage, Robert II of Flanders; and his half-brother Odo, who died en route. They were accompanied by the Normans Count Walter of Saint-Valery; the Counts of Montgomery and Mortagne; Girard of Gournay; Hugh of Saint-Pol; the sons of Hugh of Grantmesnil, who had been with William in 1066; and knights from England, Scotland, and Brittany. Passing through Rome and the Norman kingdoms of Italy, the first contingent reached Constantinople around the same time as southern Normans who had left directly for the East. The Normans were astonished by the richness of the city of Constantinople and by Emperor Alexius's generous bestowal of coins and silks. "Your father, my love," Stephen of Blois wrote to his wife, Adela, William the Conqueror's daughter, "made many great gifts, but he was almost nothing compared to this man."

Norman crusaders on their way to the Holy Land were joined by their southern cousins and in-laws, Tancred and William of Hauteville, Richard and Rainolf of Salerno, Count Geoffrey of Rissognuolo, Robert of Ansa, Herman of Cannae, Humphrey of Monte Scabioso, Albered of Cagnano, Bishop Girard of Ariano, and Bohemond of Taranto, who is said, upon hearing of the opportunity of crusade in the East, to have torn his most precious cloak in order to make scarlet crosses for those who would follow him. Bohemond's army of Normans from southern Italy and Sicily were met by Robert of Sourdeval and Beol of Chartres, Normans from Normandy.

Bohemond had fought with his father, Robert Guiscard, in their invasion of Greece in 1081. He knew the terrain better than most of the crusading chiefs, and when he arrived at Constantinople on April 9, 1097, he requested in a private audience with Emperor Alexius Comnenus to be made grand domestic of the

East, a post that would have given him authority over land seized from the heathens. Alexius demurred but managed to extract Bohemond's promise not to keep any territory taken from the Turks, an oath Bohemond would break in 1098 when he captured and became Prince of Antioch. In the biography of her father, Anna Comnena claims that "the sight of Bohemond inspired admiration, the mention of his name terror."

"Our men were all, for the first time, collected together in this place, and who could count such a great army of Christians?" writes one of Bohemond's vassals in an account of the First Crusade, the *Gesta Francorum,* of the combined armies of the West before the Seldjuk capital of Nicaea. "Then Bohemond took up his station in front of the city, then Tancred next to him, then Duke Godfrey and the Count of Flanders, next to whom was Robert of Normandy, and then the Count of Saint-Gilles and the bishop of Le Puy." The unity of the heads of diverse states before a besieged city in the East has meaning in light of all that we have understood thus far about the intention behind the making of the Bayeux Tapestry and its binding social effects.

CHAPTER 8

AN
ASYLUM
OF NOBLES

IN THE WAKE OF WILLIAM'S VICTORY AT HASTINGS, NOBLES who had either escaped the battlefield or not been there in the first place retreated to London. There, in the phrase of Orderic Vitalis, "Stigand, archbishop of Canterbury, the great earls, Edwin and Morcar, and other lords of England elected as their king Edgar Clito, son of Edward king of the Hungarians, son of Edmund called Ironside." As the grandson of Edmund Ironside, the half-brother of Edward the Confessor, Edgar was the last of Cerdic's line and the last hope for an Anglo-Saxon succession. Indeed, among all who fought to be king in 1066—Harold God-wineson, his brother Tostig, the Norwegian Harald Hardråda, and Duke William of Normandy—Edgar Æthling was, as the name Æthling denotes, the most "throne-worthy," the one with the most legitimate claim by blood. Leaving aside whatever promise Edward the Confessor may have made to William of Normandy and anything he might have said upon his deathbed, William's claim to the throne of England was less strong than that of Edgar Æthling: King Edward's mother, Emma, was William's great-aunt. Harold's claim by blood was nonexistent, despite the fact that his sister Edith was married to Edward. "Earl Harold succeeded to the kingdom of England as the king granted it to him and as he was elected thereto," states the Anglo-Saxon Laud Chronicle for the year 1066. Yet Edgar's coronation after the Battle of Hastings was the purest folly; the walls of London, which protected his court from the reality of William's advance through Kent toward the capital, were the walls of an asylum for nobles under the delusion that the realm was still theirs.

William's progress from Hastings to London was neither easy nor rapid. He waited for five days to rest and for the submission of English nobles. When none was forthcoming, he moved against Dover and advanced upon Canterbury, which surrendered before the end of October. There William's troops were slowed by the spread of dysentery, and it was not until the end of November that he gained control over most of southeast England. When able to march again, the Normans made a first assault upon London, fighting Edgar Æthling's troops at the south end of London Bridge before moving to the west and capturing Hampshire and Berkshire. William headed north, crossed the Thames at Wallingford, and isolated the capital. Archbishop Stigand came out of London to surrender at Wallingford, and at Berkhamstead, according to the Anglo-Saxon Worcester Chronicle, William "was met by bishop Ealdred, prince Edgar, earl Edwin, earl Morcar, and all the best men from London, who submitted from force of circumstances, but only when the depredation was complete."

Thus the conquest of England was hardly over at the end of the day of October 14, 1066. Though Harold was dead, William faced continued resistance not only by the handful of nobles and churchmen grouped around Edgar Æthling in London, but by Scandinavians in areas formerly ruled by men from the North and, ultimately, by Normans and Bretons William had subdued before the Conquest and who sought to escape the Norman yoke in Normandy when conditions seemed ripe. King William managed to suppress the revolt of Erdric the Wild, aided by Welch princes, in Herefordshire and, surprisingly, betrayal by Eustache of Boulogne, who in 1067 occupied briefly the town of Dover, though he had fought with the Normans at Hastings only a year

before. At the end of 1067, William was obliged to put down a re-
volt in the city of Exeter along with a second uprising of Edgar
Æthling, King Malcolm of Scotland, and the northern earls
Edwin and Morcar, who had faced Harald Hardråda at the Battle
of Fulford Gate. On January 28, 1069, William's representative
Robert of Commines, dispatched to quell the trouble in the
North, was burned to death in the bishop's house at Durham. A
bitter revolt in Northumbria in the spring of 1080 would again
culminate in the massacre of William's appointed bishop
Walcher.

English resistance to Norman occupation was compounded
by Scandinavian threats in the area—the Danelaw—with long-
standing Scandinavian affinities. In 1069, Danish king Sweyn
sent a force of 240 ships under his sons Harold and Cnut, a fleet
almost as large as that of Harald Hardråda in 1066. The Danes
captured York on September 20, 1069, and the specter of a combined Danish and Anglo-Saxon resistance loose in the land
sparked revolts in Dorset, Somerset, Staffordshire, and South
Cheshire. In 1070, Sweyn himself crossed to England, where he
was joined by a Lincolnshire thane named Hereward. Together
they harried the coast of East Anglia, looting Peterborough
Abbey, until William bribed the Danes to leave. After Sweyn's
death, his son Cnut II again arrived on the coast of England in
1075 with 200 ships and a host of Danish chiefs.

William's presence and the use of his military resources to
suppress continued resistance in England had the effect of provoking revolt at home against his rule in regions he had subdued
before the Conquest. In 1069, he put down a revolt in the town
of Le Mans in which Norman rule in Maine was contested; and in
Brittany between 1075 and 1077, an alliance between English,
French, and Scandinavians threatened for a while to unite his
deadliest enemies. The castle of Dol, taken by siege in Tapestry
panel 47 by William's and Harold's forces combined, fell to

William's opposition in 1076. The revolt of those of Brittany and on the Norman border with Brittany, encouraged by the French king, was compounded by the periodic betrayal of William's eldest son, Robert "Curthose," who managed to defeat his father's forces outside the castle of Gerberoi at the end of 1078—this in addition to the troubles with Odo that led William to imprison his half-brother in 1082. Robert revolted again in 1083, leaving the duchy and serving the French king against William until his father's death. In the decades following the Norman Conquest, the duchy and kingdom assembled by William were under constant threat of becoming unraveled. Indeed, Orderic Vitalis reports that in the speech delivered on his deathbed, William complains: "If the Normans are disciplined under a just and firm rule, they are men of great valor. . . . But without such rule they tear each other to pieces and destroy themselves, for they hanker after rebellion, cherish sedition, and are ready for any treachery." "He had much labour," observes the poet Robert Wace almost a hundred years later, "and many a war before he could hold the land in peace."

The Bayeux Tapestry is the aesthetic expression of the wish to hold the kingdom and duchy together, "to hold the land in peace." A meeting place upon a single visual plane of the diverse parties to the events of 1066 and their aftermath, the Tapestry interweaves elements associated with Anglo-Saxon, Scandinavian, and Norman culture. And in this way, the surface of the textile expresses a desire for reconciliation among the principals to a bitter and extended struggle. The story it tells is, of course, that of a great Norman victory, and it tells it in such a visually forceful way that the viewer is compelled to see and to believe that history could not have turned out otherwise. Yet the Tapestry's visual narrative does not participate in the vindictiveness for which

William the Conqueror was famed when he felt that he or his men had been wronged. On the contrary, it is various and inclusive; and the very unresolved nature of understandings of such a complex work of art shows, finally, how wide the spectrum of those who can identify with it, how wide its appeal, really is. That history is written, or embroidered, on the side of the victor is no secret. But the Tapestry does not crushingly espouse one side of the struggle against the other. It is both Anglo-Saxon and Norman, or, in the terms by which nineteenth-century nationalists and historians have judged it, it is both English and French—with a large contribution from Scandinavia. All-embracing, the Tapestry works in a manner similar to that of Orderic Vitalis, when he expresses his own desire to "record without distortion the chances and changes of English and Normans alike. . . . I look to neither victors nor vanquished," says Orderic, "for the honour of any reward."

The Bayeux Tapestry is inclusive, and it leaves important issues such as the reasons for Harold's trip to Normandy, the nature of his oath, and the specifics of Edward's deathbed legacy sufficiently undefined as to permit all to identify with their particular point of view. It is the artistic embodiment of a pluralism within the sphere of social relations, giving expression to competing claims to England, while working toward a synthesis by which they might converge at some moment in the future. A suture for the wound of 1066, the Tapestry expresses the will for a weaving together of England and Normandy under the more or less constant threat of coming apart in the decades after the Conquest.

The inclusion of Oriental elements within the mix may be surprising, yet they serve precisely the same unifying purpose by focusing Anglo-Saxon and Norman claims upon a common third term. Relations with Byzantium are inscribed in the Bayeux Tapestry both within and all along its edges as a desire to participate in the prestige of the East and a desire to possess. The Tapestry can be said, as has been claimed more generally of the Crusades, to channel the energies of quarrelsome European knights in the cause of a just war against an enemy from without. In the sermon preached at Clermont in 1095, Pope Urban II, in the phrase of Orderic Vitalis, "urged the nobles of the west and their men and companions to make a lasting peace among themselves, . . . and as renowned lords, prove the valour of their knighthood against the pagans." The exotic animals and designs in the margins can be taken as an expansion of the war story contained in the main panels beyond its borders, just as the Crusades can be seen as a continuation of Norman ambitions beyond southern Italy, Sicily, and England. The uniting of Normans from Anglo-Normandy and the South in the undertaking of further conquest is written into the Tapestry some fifteen years before it will become historical fact.

The capacity to reflect and to shape the world around it makes the Bayeux Tapestry a great and enduring work of art—and a singularly medieval one. Like the first Old French epics with which it is roughly contemporaneous and that recount the struggle against the pagans, the Tapestry is a collaborative work, involving Anglo-Saxons and Normans and meant for open display, whether in a great palace, a cathedral, or even outdoors. The Tapestry, unlike, say, an illuminated prayer book or precious piece of jewelry, is a public work of art that gives expression to shared dilemmas and works collectively toward their solution.

The great secular works of art of the High Middle Ages, whether epic songs, the first courtly romances, or the Bayeux Tapestry, are filled with legal issues—scenes of council, disputes over succession, trials, oaths, and vengeful executions. They are intended to encourage loyalty and to condemn betrayal, to foster communal values and vision, to elicit complicity between maker and viewer, and to do so even before such unity becomes embodied in institutions. The Tapestry offers a fine example of art anticipating life, of art making life in times not yet ready for the kind of social and political healing its culturally mixed embroidered surface entails. The Anglo-Norman unity held in place by the economic apparatus of the Exchequer; the judicial institutions of written laws, trial by inquest, and appeal; and the political trappings of an efficiently administrative state will not come about until the reign of William the Conqueror's son Henry I (ruled 1100–1135) and his grandson Henry II (ruled 1154–1189), for whom the story of the Norman Conquest was, in the phrase of Henry of Huntington, writing around the middle of the twelfth century, "a change in the right hand of God."

Part of what makes the Tapestry so fascinating is that it rides the cusp of one of the great moments of transformation the West has ever known. Even if we cannot say with certainty who commissioned it, where it was made, by whom, and for what purpose, we can still appreciate at over nine centuries' remove the ways it both reflects and participates in historical change. Understood as pointing to the future as well as the past, as a window of dreams that will come true because they carry real social and political yearnings, it yields a founding vision of what will become the Anglo-Norman world. The Bayeux Tapestry is simply the best picture we have of the Norman Conquest and of the beginnings of feudalism in the West. In this, it is no different from many great works—the friezes of Nineveh for ancient Assyria, vases for Greece, Trajan's Column for Rome, Leonardo's "Vitruvian Man" for the Renaissance, Picasso's *Demoiselles d'Avignon* for the modern era—that both chart and define our image of an age.

ACKNOWLEDGMENTS

I would like to thank my graduate students at Yale for all they brought to the seminar table, and the J. Paul Getty Trust for a delicious year among the colleagues and books of the Getty Research Institute, Los Angeles.

NOTES

PREFACE

1. Manuscript 199 in the departmental archives of Calvados at Caen, Normandy, titled "Inventory of the Treasury of the Cathedral, 1476" contains the following entry: "Item, a very long and narrow linen embroidered with images and writing, representing the conquest of England, which is suspended around the nave of the church the day and throughout the Octave of Relics." (Republished in Shirley Ann Brown, *The Bayeux Tapestry: History and Bibliography* [Suffolk: Boydell Press, 1988], appendix I, A, p. 161.)

CHAPTER 2: PERILS AND SURVIVAL

1. For an account of Hitler's attempt to capture the Tacitus *Germania,* see Simon Schama, *Landscape and Memory* (New York: Vintage Books, 1995), pp. 75–81.

2. Sylvette Lemagnen, "L'Histoire de la Tapisserie de Bayeux à l'heure allemande," in *La Tapisserie de Bayeux: L'art de broder l'Histoire,* eds. Pierre Bouet, Brian Levy, François Neveux (Caen: Presses Universitaires de Caen, 2004), pp. 53–54. This article is the major source of knowledge about the Jankuhn mission.

3. This journal was presented to the Centre Guillaume le Conquérant in Bayeux on November 18, 1994, by Jankuhn's widow and son.

4. See Shirley Ann Brown, "The History of the Bayeux Tapestry," in *The Bayeux Tapestry: History and Bibliography* (Suffolk: Boydell Press, 1988), pp. 18–19.

5. René Dubosq, *La Tapisserie de Bayeux: Dix années tragiques de sa longue histoire* (Caen: Ozanne et Cie., 1951), pp. 50–63.

6. Von Choltitz, "Pourquoi, en 1944, je n'ai pas détruit Paris," *Le Figaro,* October 12, 1949, p. 5.

7. Paul Chutkow, "Update: The Bayeux Tapestry Still Smells," *Connoisseur* 213 (March 1983): 18.

8. *Mémoires de littérature tirés des registres de l'Académie Royale des Inscriptions et Belles-Lettres,* vol. 6 (Amsterdam: François Changuion, 1729), p. 739.

9. The sources for the history of the Tapestry, which I have used as a guide, are Simone Bertrand, "The History of the Tapestry," in Frank Stenton, *The Bayeux Tapestry: A Comprehensive Survey* (Greenwich, Conn., Phaidon: 1957), pp. 88–97; and the more detailed Shirley Ann Brown, *The Bayeux Tapestry: History and Bibliography* (Suffolk: Boydell Press, 1988), pp. 1–44. The suggestion that Anne Foucault made the drawings is contained in Aase Luplau Janssen, "La Redécouverte de la Tapisserie de Bayeux," *Annales de Normandie* 11 (October 1961): 179–95.

10. "La Conquête de l'Angleterre par Guillaume le Bâtard, Duc de Normandie, dit le Conquérant," *Les Monumens de la Monarchie Françoise,* vol. 2 (Paris: Gandouin et Giffart, 1730), pp. 1–31.

11. Bertrand, "History," pp. 90–91.

12. Visconti, *Notice historique sur la Tapisserie brodée de la reine Mathilde, épouse de Guillaume le Conquérant* (Paris, Imprimerie des Sciences et Arts, 1803).

13. John Collingwood Bruce, *The Bayeux Tapestry: The Battle of Hastings and the Norman Conquest* (New York: Dorset Press, 1987; first published 1856), p. 17.

14. "Some Observations on the Bayeux Tapestry," *Archaeologica* 19 (1821): 185.

15. The well-known editor, historian, and literary specialist Achille Jubinal accused Stothard of removing the piece ("Tapisserie de Bayeux," *L'Artiste,* first series, vol. 12 [1836]: 42–44); the return of the piece is detailed by Ernest Lefébure ("A Propos de la Tapisserie de Bayeux," *La Chronique des Arts et de la Curiosité* 35 [October 10, 1872]: 357–58); and Mrs. Stothard's nephew exonerates her in a letter to the *London Times* (Charles N. Kempe, "The Bayeux Tapestry," *London Times,* September 24, 1881, p. 10).

16. Mildred Budny, "The Byrhtnoth Tapestry or Embroidery," in *The Battle of Maldon,* ed. Donald Scragg (Oxford: Basil Blackwell, 1991), pp. 263–79.

17. Despite the mention of hangings dedicated to religious institutions, few of which have survived, we know next to nothing about their size or whether they were decorative or put to liturgical use as, say, altar coverings or clerical vestments.

18. Simone Bertrand, *La Tapisserie de Bayeux et la manière de vivre au onzième siècle* (Saint-Leger-Vauban, Yonne: Zodiaque, 1966), p. 12.

19. *The Cistercians: Monastic Writings of the Twelfth Century,* ed. Pauline Matarasso (New York: Penguin, 1993), p. 57.

20. *Beowulf,* tr. Seamus Heaney (New York: Farrar, Straus & Giroux, 2000), v. 994.

21. Richard Brilliant, "The Bayeux Tapestry: A Stripped Narrative for Their Eyes and Ears," in Richard Gameson, *The Study of the Bayeux Tapestry* (Woodbridge: Boydell Press, 1997), p. 118.

22. *Anglo-Saxon Poetic Records,* vol. 3 (New York: Columbia University Press, 1931–1953), p. 159.

23. G. I. Christie, *English Medieval Embroidery* (Oxford: Clarendon Press, 1938), appendix I, pp. 31–32; C. R. Dodwell, *Anglo-Saxon Art: A New Perspective* (Ithaca: Cornell University Press, 1982), pp. 57–72.

24. Cited, David J. Bernstein, *The Mystery of the Bayeux Tapestry* (London: Weidenfeld & Nicolson, 1986), p. 200.

25. The case for Samur is made in a recent book by George Beech, *Was the Bayeux Tapestry Made in France?* (New York: Palgrave Macmillan, 2005).

CHAPTER 3: WAR BY OTHER MEANS

1. Quoted in Dorothy Doolittle, "The Relations Between Literature and Mediaeval Studies in France from 1820 to 1860" (dissertation: Bryn Mawr College, 1933), p. 98. Cited, William Roach, "Francisque Michel: A Pioneer in Medieval Studies," *Proceedings of the American Philosophical Society* 114, no. 3 (June 1970): 169.

2. Harry Redman Jr., *The Roland Legend in Nineteenth-Century French Literature* (Lexington: University Press of Kentucky, 1991), p. 77.

3. *Journal des débats* (January 8, 1814); Chateaubriand, *Oeuvres complètes,* vol. 9 (Paris: Garnier, 1859), p. 440.

4. Cited, Joseph Bédier, "De L'Edition princeps de la *Chanson de Roland* aux éditions les plus récentes," *Romania* 63 (1937): 448.

5. *Archaelogia* 12 (1796): 299, 76.

6. Letter cited in Bédier, "Edition princeps," p. 458.

7. Cited in Laurent Thies, "Guizot et les Institutions de Mémoire" in *Les Lieux de Mémoire,* vol. 2, ed. Pierre Nora (Paris: Gallimard, 1997), p. 580.

8. Ibid., p. 588.

9. *Chronique des Ducs de Normandie par Benoit, trouvère Anglo-Normand du XIIe siècle,* vol. I (Paris: Imprimerie Royale, 1836), p. ii.

10. "La *Chanson de Roland* et la nationalité française," in *La poésie du moyen âge* (Paris; Hachette, 1913), p. 118.

11. Léon Gautier, *Les Epopées françaises: Étude sur les origines et l'histoire de la littérature nationale* (Paris: Librairie Universitaire, 1892), p. 749.

12. *L'armée à travers les âges: Conférences faites en 1900* (Paris, 1902), cited in Andrew Taylor, "Was There a *Song of Roland?" Speculum* 76 (2001): 36.

13. Cited in Claudine I. Wilson, "A Frenchman in England: Francisque Michel," *Revue de littérature comparée* 17 (1937): 740.

14. "De la Manière d'écrire l'histoire en France et en Allemagne depuis cinquante ans," *Revue des deux mondes* 101 (1872): 245. See also Maurice Wilmotte, *L'Enseignement de la philologie romane à Paris et en Allemagne (1883–1885): Rapport à M. le ministre de l'intérieur et de l'instruction publique* (Bruxelles: Imprimerie Polleunis, Centerick & Lefébure, 1886), pp. 16–17.

15. "Chronique," in *Revue des Questions Historiques* 9 (1870): 496.

16. Gabriel Monod, *Allemands et français: Souvenirs de campagne* (Paris: Sandoz et Fischbacher, 1872), p. 39; see also pp. 130, 131.

17. Paul Meyer, *Rapport sur l'état actuel de la philologie des langues romanes* (London: Transactions of the Philological Society, 1873–1874), pp. 411–12.

18. Cited in Janine Dakyns, *The Middle Ages in French Literature, 1851–1900* (Oxford: Oxford University Press, 1973), p. 34.

19. Ibid., p. 36.

20. See article "La France" by Louis Halphen in *Histoire et historiens depuis cinquante ans: Méthodes, organisations et résultats du travail historique de 1876 à 1926; recueil publié à l'occasion du cinquantenaire de la* Revue historique (Paris: Félix Alcan, 1927), pp. 148–67.

21. Stephanie L. Barczewski, *Myth and National Identity in Nineteenth-Century Britain: The Legends of King Arthur and Robin Hood* (Oxford: Oxford University Press, 2000), p. 30.

22. *England and Spain; or, Valour and Patriotism* (London: T. Cadell and W. Davies, 1808), p. 7.

23. Sir Walter Scott, *Ivanhoe* (New York: Random House, 2001), pp. 287, 8, 4.

24. See Barczewski, *Myth and National Identity,* p. 34.

25. Thomas Carlyle, *Chartism* (London: Chapman & Hill, 1890), p. 45.

26. Jules Michelet, *Le Moyen Age,* (Paris: Robert Laffont, 2000), p. 221.

27. Thomas Arnold, *Introductory Lectures on Modern History* (Oxford: J. H. Parker, 1842), p. 30.

28. According to Philippa Levine in *The Amateur and the Professional: Antiquarians, Historians, and Archaeologists in Victorian England, 1838–1886* (New York: Cambridge University Press, 1986), p. 179.

29. Frederick Dixon, "The Round Table," *The Temple Bar* 109 (1896): 210.

30. *The Queen's Reign and Its Commemoration, 1837–97* (London: Warner, 1897), p. 60.

31. Chateaubriand, *Génie du Christianisme* (Paris: Imprimerie Mignaret, 1803), p. 153; Victor Hugo, "La Bande noire," in *Oeuvres poétiques,* vol. i (Paris: Pléiade, 1964), p. 342.

CHAPTER 4: A STITCH IN TIME

1. William of Malmesbury, *Gesta Regum Anglorum,* ed. Roger Mynors, vol. I (Oxford: Clarendon Press, 1998), book 3, p. 451.

2. "A Swallow and Other Birds," in Aesop, *Fables* (New York: Dover Publications, 1967), pp. 64–65.

3. Marie de France, *Fables,* ed. Harriet Spiegel (Toronto: University of Toronto Press, 1994), p. 77.

4. Cited in Agnes Geijer, *A History of Textile Art* (London: Pasold Research Fund, 1979), p. 77.

5. The technical analysis that follows is based upon Marie-Hélène Didier, "La Broderie, une oeuvre textile: Les expertises et les analyses effectuées en 1982–1983; la mise en place de l'opération," and Isabelle Bédat and Béatrice Girault-Kurtzeman, "Etude technique de la Broderie de Bayeux," in *La Tapisserie de Bayeux: L'art de broder l'histoire,* eds. Pierre Bouet, Brian Levy, and François Neveux (Caen: Presses Universitaires de Caen, 2004), pp. 77–82, 83–109.

6. One wonders why the Tapestry's wool is not tested by radiocarbon methods to determine the date of the embroidery itself. One might also contemplate DNA testing of the wool, in conjunction with sheep bones buried in the ground of the most likely sites of its making, to supplement the scientific determination of time with that of place.

7. M. L. Ryder, *Sheep and Man* (London: Duckworth, 1983), p. 185.

8. William Stubbs, *Memorials of St. Dunstan* (London: Rolls Series, 1874), pp. 20–21.

9. Agnes Strickland, *Lives of the Queens of England,* vol. I (London: Henry Colburn, 1851), p. 65.

10. For a description of the techniques of embroidery, see George Wingfield Digby, "Technique and Production," in Frank Stenton, *The Bayeux Tapestry: A Comprehensive Survey* (Greenwich, Conn.: Phaidon, 1957), pp. 37–55; Simone Bertrand, *La Tapisserie de Bayeux et la manière de vivre au onzième siècle* (Saint-Leger-Vauban, Yonne: Zodiaque, 1966), pp. 23–32; Bédat and Girault-Kurtzeman, "Etude Technique."

11. Hudson Gurney, "Observations on the Bayeux Tapestry," *Archaeologia* 18 (1817): 359; Thomas Frognall Dibdin, *A Bibliographic, Antiquarian and Picturesque Tour in France and Germany* (London: Robert Jennings & John Major, 1829), p. 247.

12. See Richard Brilliant, "The Bayeux Tapestry: A Stripped Narrative for Their Eyes and Ears," in Richard Gameson, *The Study of the Bayeux Tapestry* (Woodbridge: Bydell Press, 1997), pp. 125ff.

CHAPTER 5: BURIED TREASURE

1. "Basil Brown's Diary of the Excavations at Sutton Hoo in 1938–39," in Rupert Bruce-Mitford, *Aspects of Anglo-Saxon Archaeology: Sutton Hoo and Other Discoveries* (New York: Harper's Magazine Press, 1974), p. 146.

2. Sutton Hoo Archive X2/3.4. Cited in Martin Carver, *Sutton Hoo: Burial Ground of Kings?* (London: British Museum Press, 1998), p. 5.

3. Bruce-Mitford, *Anglo-Saxon Archaeology,* p. 161.

4. As reported by Robert Markham, *Sutton Hoo Through the Rear View Mirror, 1937–1942* (Woodbridge, Suffolk: Sutton Hoo Society, 2002), p. 22.

5. A report on the inquest regarding treasure trove is to be found in Rupert Bruce-Mitford, *The Sutton Hoo Ship-Burial,* vol. I (London: British Museum, 1975), pp. 719–25.

6. Cited in Peter Anker, *The Art of Scandinavia,* vol. I (London: Paul Hamlyn, 1970), p. 60.

7. See Lucien Musset, *La Tapisserie de Bayeux* (Paris: Zodiaque, 2002), p. 20; David M. Wilson and Ole Klindt-Jensen, *Viking Art* (Minneapolis: University of Minneapolis Press, 1963), pp. 82–83.

8. *King Harald's Saga,* tr. Magnus Magnusson (New York: Penguin, 1984), p. 111.

9. Ibid., p. 108

10. Wolfgang Grape, *The Bayeux Tapestry: Monument to a Norman Triumph* (Munich and New York: Prestel, 1994), p. 64.

11. Agnes Strickland, *Lives of the Queens of England,* vol. I (London: Henry Colburn, 1851), p. 66.

12. The edition used is that of Harriet Spiegel, *The Fables of Marie de France* (Toronto: University of Toronto Press, 1994).

13. *The Alexiad of Anna Comnena,* tr. E. R. A. Sewter (London: Penguin Books, 1969), p. 360.

CHAPTER 6: WEAVING TO BYZANTIUM

1. Snorri Sturluson, *Harald's Saga,* tr. Magnus Magnusson and Hermann Pálsson (New York: Penguin Books, 1984), p. 48.

2. Michael Psellus, *Fourteen Byzantine Rulers: The Chronographia of Michael Psellus,* tr. E. R. A. Sewter (Baltimore: Penguin Books, 1966), p. 91.

3. *The Alexiad of Anna Comnena,* tr. E. R. A. Sewter (London: Penguin Books, 1969), p. 95.

4. *Njal's Saga,* tr. Magnus Magnusson and Hermann Pálsson (Baltimore: Penguin books, 1964), p. 176.

5. Lucien Musset, *Introduction à la runologie* (Paris: Aubier-Montaigne, 1965).

6. Orderic Vitalis, *The Ecclesiastical History,* vol. II, ed. Marjorie Chibnall (Oxford: Clarendon Press, 1969), p. 143.

7. Ibid.

8. Sturluson, *Harald's Saga,* p. 138.

9. William of Poitiers, *Gesta Guillelmi,* eds. Marjorie Chibnall and R. H. C. Davis (Oxford: Clarendon Press, 1998), p. 111.

10. Guy of Amiens, *Carmen de Hastengae Proelio,* eds. Catherine Morton and Hope Muntz (Oxford: Clarendon Press, 1972), p. 7.

11. Michael Hendy, "Michael IV and Harald Hardråda," *The Numismatic Chronicles* 10 (series 7, 1970): 187–97.

12. Adam of Bremen III, 52, Schol, 83, see Hilda R. Davidson, *The Viking Road to Byzantium* (London: George Allen, 1976), pp. 227–28.

13. Guy of Amiens, *Carmen de Hastengae Proelio,* p. 13.

14. These examples are taken from Anna Muthesius, *Byzantine Silk Weaving* A.D. *400 to* A.D. *1200* (Vienna: Fassbaender, 1997), p. 125.

15. Robert S. Lopez, "Silk Industry in the Byzantine Empire," *Speculum* 20 (1945): 28.

16. *Laxaedala Saga,* tr. Magnus Magnusson and Hermann Pálsson (Baltimore: Penguin Books, 1969), p. 236.

CHAPTER 7: GO EAST, YOUNG NORMAN

1. David C. Douglas, *William the Conqueror* (Berkeley: University of California Press, 1967), p. 266.

2. The quotation is contained in Orderic Vitalis, *Ecclesiastical History,* vol. II, ed. Marjorie Chibnall (Oxford: Oxford University Press, 1969), p. 203.

3. The figure of 350 ships is given in the Icelandic *Saga of Edward the Confessor* published in the Rolls Series 88, vol. III (London: Public Records Office, 1894), pp. 424–28.

4. Lynn White, *Medieval Technology* (London: Oxford University Press, 1962), p. 37.

5. Guy of Amiens, *Carmen de Hastengae Proelio,* p. 25.

6. O. K. Werckmeister, "The Political Ideology of the Bayeux Tapestry," *Studi medievali* 17 (1976): 540.

7.   Amatus of Montecassino, *The History of the Normans,* eds. Prescott N. Dunbar and Graham A. Loud (Suffolk: Boydell Press, 2004), p. 50.

8.   Bernard S. Bachrach, "Some Observations on the Military Administration of the Norman Conquest," *Anglo-Norman Studies* 8 (1985): 1–25.

INDEX

Page numbers in *italics* refer to illustrations.

ABOUT THE AUTHOR

R. HOWARD BLOCH is the Sterling Professor of French and the Director of the Humanities Division at Yale University. He is the author of numerous books about the Middle Ages, including *The Anonymous Marie de France*, winner of the 2004 Aldo and Jeanne Scaglione Prize of the Modern Language Association.

ABOUT THE TYPE

This book was set in Requiem, a typeface designed by the Hoefler Type Foundry. It is a modern typeface inspired by inscriptional capitals in Ludovico Vicentino degli Arrighi's 1523 writing manual, *Il modo de temperare le penne*. An original lowercase, a set of figures, and an italic in the "chancery" style that Arrighi helped popularize were created to make this adaptation of a classical design into a complete font family.